COFFEE WITH PLEASURE

COFFEE WITH PLEASURE

PLEASURE

JUST JAVA AND WORLD TRADE

LAURE WARIDEL

Montréal/New York
London

Black Rose Books No. EE305

Canadian Cataloguing in Publication Data

Waridel, Laure
Coffee with pleasure : just java and world trade

Includes bibliographical references.
Paperback ISBN: 1-55164-190-9 (pbk.) Hardcover ISBN: 1-55164-191-7 (bound)

1. Coffee industry--Mexico. 2. Coffee industry--Social aspects--Mexico. I. Title.
HD9199.M42W363 2001   382'.41373'0972   C00-901401-2

Cover design by KO création
Interior by Amélie Binette
Photographs by Éric St-Pierre

BLACK ROSE BOOKS

C.P. 1258	2250 Military Road	99 Wallis Road
Succ. Place du Parc	Tonawanda, NY	London, E9 5LN
Montréal, H2W 2R3	14150	England
Canada	USA	UK

To order books:
In Canada:
(phone) 1-800-565-9523 (fax) 1-800-221-9985 email: utpbooks@utpress.utoronto.ca

In United States:
(phone) 1-800-283-3572 (fax) 1-651-917-6406

In the UK & Europe:
(phone) London 44 (0)20 8986-4854 (fax) 44 (0)20 8533-5821 email: order@centralbooks.com

Our Web Site address: www.web.net/blackrosebooks

The Canada Council   Le Conseil des Arts
for the Arts   du Canada

A publication of the Institute of Policy Alternatives of Montréal (IPAM)

We thank the Canadian International Development Agency (CIDA) for its support.

Printed in Canada on recycled paper

For Adela,
Felix, Rosanalia
and all the coffee growers
who have inspired these lines.

In the name of justice.

*At the time of going to press,
world coffee prices were well below
the cost of production.*

Contents

Foreword

You hold in your hands a rare treasure. *Coffee with Pleasure* is part dream, whole practical, a book about hope and life and ethics. It is the story of a cause and of a movement and it builds a bridge of promise to tomorrow for millions of workers and their families around the world.

Free trade is the problem. Fair trade is the solution. Currently world trade is dominated by the ideology of economic globalization—the creation of a single global economy with universal rules set by big business for big business in which a seamless global consumer market operates on free-market principles, unfettered by domestic or international laws or standards. This system of trade is controlled by a handful of transnational corporations operating outside any domestic law or any international rules except business-friendly trade agreements. And it is creating deep and entrenched inequalities in its wake.

The combined sales income of the world's top 200 transnational corporations amount to almost twice the annual income of the bottom four-fifths of humanity. Eighty countries have lower per-capita incomes today than they did a decade or more ago and 200 million more people this year are living in absolute poverty (on less than $1 a day). The world's 225 richest individuals have a combined income equal to the annual income of half of humanity. The world's three richest men—Bill Gates and his two partners in Microsoft—have a combined annual income greater than the combined income of the 48 least developed countries!

The current coffee trade is a perfect example of this corrupt system. A handful of giant agro-food corporations dominate the trade, raking in huge profits and leaving in their wake underpaid workers, chemical pollution and impoverished communities. With every passing year, their grip on the sector tightens and the return to the workers and their families diminishes.

There is an alternative. Growing alongside an awakening global population is the concept of fair trade—that in our role as consumers and coffee lovers, we can build an equitable world trading system, one in which those who toiled to bring us our liquid pleasure work in safe conditions, enjoy democratic rights and provide for their families and their communities.

Coffee with Pleasure is chock-full of information; you'll find out all you need to know to become a fair-trade coffee drinker and promoter. But it is also filled with the stories of real people struggling to build a dream. You can almost reach through the pages of this book and touch them. So sit down, pour yourself a cup of deliciously brewed, lovingly made, fairly rewarded fair-trade coffee and dip into this treasure. You won't be sorry.

Maude Barlow
National Chairperson of the Council of Canadians
and a Director with the International Forum on Globalization.

Acknowledgments

IN MEXICO...

I wish to thank all the members of the *Unión de Communidades Indigenas de la Región del Istmo* (UCIRI) for helping me to learn about and better understand coffee and fair trade. Thank you for opening the door to your daily life, and for sharing the roof over your head. Thanks to the women, who taught me to make tortillas, wash my ideas in the river along with my clothes, and carry a mountain of wood, and who gave me a mountain of inspiration. A special *gracias* to the members of UCIRI's Board of Directors at the time Éric St-Pierre and I visited in 1996: Rey Hernández Chávez, Victorino Terán Jiménez, Celestino Cortéz Monterrubio and Constantino Galván Toledo; to the entire team at the peasant education centre: Ubelia Altamirano Escobar, Guadalupe Quiroz Jiménez, Hanneke Kruit, Armida Sánchez López, Hernán Martínez Morales, Juliesa Cabrera Vásquez, Jesús Antonio Ramírez and their inspiring students; *gracias* to Rosanelia, Lilia Cruz Altamirano, Gregorio De Anda, Adela Gusmán López, José Eli Jiménez Orozco, Aurora Juarez, Feliciano and Juana Modesta Cheto, Isaías Martínez Morales, Félix Terán Mendoza, Roberto Raygoza, Frank Vanderhoff and Clerserio Villanueva; and to all those who are not mentioned by name but whose smiles and frowns inspired the following pages. *Ish Guich.*

I also owe special thanks to Jorge Parra and Rosa María Dueñas, who translated the first edition of this book (*Coffee with a Cause.* Les Intouchables, Montréal, 1997) and adapted it for Latin-American countries (*Un café por la Causa* was published by Madre Tierra in 2001). Luis Martínez Villanueva and Chloée Campero also played an important role in bringing that project to fruition. Their knowledge and perspective has contributed to *Coffee with Pleasure.* Thank you also to Erubiel Hernandez, for his wonderful work in Chiapas, and for accompanying me on my visits to large coffee estates, letting me better understand the dark side of the picture.

IN CANADA AND THE USA...

Many people helped to make this book possible, and my heart-felt thanks go to all of them. Without the support of Stephen Jones, my indefatigable editor and *franglais* decoder, I would not have taken on the job of revising, extending and improving the first edition, which was little more than a booklet. *Diolch yn fawr,* Stephen! I must thank Éric St-Pierre, who suggested the initial research trip that grew into Équiterre's A Just Coffee campaign. He took the exquisite photographs which you can see in this book and wrote the sidebar on indigenous peoples. François Meloche contributed to the sixth chapter, Jackie Kirk wrote the sidebar on birds, and Boris-Antoine Legault and Towagh Behr provided research assistance: *Merci !* Thanks to Noah Chaikel, Claire Heenan, and Stephen Jones for their work in translating the first edition from French into English, and to Heather Leighton and Peter Feldstein for translating passages from the Spanish edition.

Thanks to Sara Teitelbaum for her work on the research report on fair trade in Europe that we wrote jointly and which provided a good deal of information for the sixth chapter and the appendixes. Sasha Courville freely shared with me information that is the fruit of many years of doctoral research and study. Thank you to Bob Thomson for his endless support and valuable suggestions for improvements. The comments and collaboration of: Rodney North and Erbin Crowell of Equal Exchange; Heather

Weinrich and Caroline Witby of Transfair Canada; Zachary Patterson and Janice Astbury of the Commission for Environmental Cooperation; Patrick Mallet of Falls Brook Centre; Isabelle St-Germain, Elizabeth Hunter, Normand Roy and Sara Mayo of Équiterre; Monica Firl; Jean-Philippe Linteau; and Louis Chauvin of McGill University have been very helpful in adapting this new edition.

Thank you also to my professors at the University of Victoria, Dr. Michael M'Gonigle of the POLIS Project on Ecological Governance, Dr. Martha McMahon, and Dr. Michael Webb, for supervising the research which allowed me to write this book.

Grazie tanto to Nicolina Farrela for transforming numbers into graphs, and to Philippe Dunsky for rescuing one of the latter. This book might not have caught your attention without the fine cover by Annie Lachapelle and the page design by Amélie Binette. *Merci Amélie et Annie.*

I am grateful to Maude Barlow, of the Council of Canadians, not only for agreeing to write the foreword of this edition, but for all her tireless work on behalf of environmental and social-justice causes. Thank you to Dimitrios Roussopoulos and Linda Barton of Black Rose Books for bringing this book into your hands.

Lastly, I wish to thank all those who are working to make fair trade possible, and particularly to my colleague at Équiterre, Isabelle St-Germain, and all the volunteers involved in campaigns for fair trade and organic agriculture. They are making a difference, cup by cup.

AND IN MY HEART...
Merci à Hugo Latulippe, l'homme de ma vie!

Laure Waridel, Montréal, September 2001

Introduction
Making a Difference with Every Cup

For millions of people coffee is a pleasure, a delight for the soul or a morning pick-me-up. If we let coffee open our eyes wide enough, we can trace it all the way back to the mountains of Latin America, Africa and Asia. This book sets out to take you there via Mexico. It will show you two different paths—two routes that coffee can take to get to you—so that you can better choose which one you want to favour when you take a cup of Java.

The main coffee route, the highway for most of the coffee that we drink, is the legacy of the colonial past. Coffee is bought at the cheapest price and resold at the highest along a long chain of intermediaries. On this route social and environmental issues are not factored into prices and thus receive little consideration. The market rules.

Coffee-plantation workers earn an average of between $1* and $3 a day, or about $1,000 a year.[1] Meanwhile, the president of Philip Morris, Geoffrey C. Bible, earned over $5 million in the year 2000.[2] His company controls many of the brands we find in supermarkets—Maxwell House, Nabob, Sanka, Yuban, General Food International Coffee, Blendy and Carte Noire, to name but a few. Such a huge disparity of conditions between people involved in the same trade calls to mind the inequities of the Middle Ages: the poor in developing countries have, in a sense, become the serfs of a

* Sums of money are in US dollars unless otherwise stated.

1

minority in the developed world. This sits oddly with the notion that we are living in the "free-market era."

The current world prices for coffee—set in New York and London—have fallen to *their lowest ever level in real terms*.[3] As I write these lines, middlemen are paying peasants in Mexico around 44 cents for a kilogram of coffee that will cost North American or European consumers at least $8 and sometimes as much as $30. Ironically, at a time when growers are in dire straits, big coffee companies are proudly announcing record profits.

Because coffee is the only source of income for many rural families, thousands of people, especially the young, are moving to towns hoping for a better life. In the streets of a little coffee town such as Motozintla, in Southern Chiapas, you can read signs like: "*Salidas a Tijuana. Pasaje 1,300 pesos. Informacion aqui.*" (Departure for Tijuana, 1,300 pesos. Information here.)

It is estimated that plantation workers are leaving at a rate of 500 families per week from the State of Chiapas alone.[4] Buses are organized to bring people all the way to the urban "free zone" near the US border, where there is work in sweatshops. The world market needs to be fed. Once so close to the US border, many have hopes of reaching the American Dream. But although goods can easily cross borders, facilitated by the North American Free Trade Agreement (NAFTA), Mexicans themselves are kept behind fences. On May 7, 2001 seven coffee farmers from Veracruz, Mexico died in the Arizona desert in an effort to escape the hopelessness of coffee growing and current world prices.[5] The American government is increasing security measures to keep people out, but freeing trade to welcome in their products. The American Dream requires a visa.

The current coffee crisis is also having an impact on the environment. Most Mexican coffee is grown in mountainous areas, where the ecological balance is already fragile. Under the canopy of the forest, coffee can be produced without using agrochemicals, more sustainably than any crop grown by intensive "monocropping" methods, such as sugarcane or maize. Sustainable production helps maintain biodiversity and the quality of the soil and prevents soil erosion. Because current coffee prices do not even cover the basic cost of production, many farmers are looking for more lucrative uses for their land. Some peasants are cutting down the forest, selling their wood and cheaply renting their land to large livestock owners. In other areas, coffee plantations are being turned into sugarcane fields.

A breach is being made in this exploitative system. In response to the negative social and environmental impacts of conventional coffee production and trading, alternatives are being developed—among them fair-trade, organic and shade-grown coffee.

Fair trade involves more than just paying a higher price for a product. It means working towards the goal of more equitable trading relationships between producers and consumers. Fair trade is based on economic justice and aims to empower local people rather than give them charity. Fair-trade coffee is bought directly from farmers' cooperatives that use small-scale, environmentally sustainable production methods. The price paid to cooperatives is higher than the world price, allowing the families not only to meet daily needs, but also to instigate projects to improve their quality of life and use agricultural methods that are respectful of the environment. They alone decide what projects they want to pursue. Most of the producers involved in fair trade also grow their coffee organically and under the shade of the forest. Another advantage of fair trade is that cooperatives can obtain cash advances and/or loans on reasonable terms from Northern partners with whom they have long-term agreements.

After reading this book, you will know a good deal more about the difference between the conventional and the fair-trade coffee routes. You will know what kind of coffee will give you the greatest pleasure, not only on account of taste and price, but also of the story behind it.

We often hear it said that "money rules the world." When we observe how "the market" influences the economy, and how the economy dictates the behaviour not only of businesses but of politicians, we see that the old adage is close to the mark. By the same token, since the global market rules over the economy and the economy commands politics, buying becomes voting.

Since little information is available about the "chain of custody" of the products we buy, and since most of us do not realize the political implications of our purchasing decisions, we are usually casting blind votes. Egged on by advertising, bargains and special offers, we buy products without thinking of—and without knowing much about—their real environmental and social costs. In our race to buy more for less, we feed the corporations that many of us denounce. In so doing, we are behaving exactly like the corporations by choosing the cheapest possible products with little heed for those who produced them, nor for their environmental impacts.

Under these circumstances, and without intervention from governments, economic power is becoming increasingly concentrated in the hands of a relatively small number of multinational corporations. New mergers and record profits for large corporations and banks are the stuff of daily news, as are massive layoffs and the displacement of operations to countries where environmental and social regulations are weakest.[6]

This is one of the reasons why, in the streets of Seattle, you could hear activists chanting "Fair trade, not free trade" during the WTO Millennium Round in November 1999. People were demonstrating for a wide range of reasons, but overall there was a common cry to make trade more sustainable for all. Reaching far beyond the sporadic demonstrations at Seattle, Québec City and Genoa, this cry is echoed and being taken up by panoply of civil-society organizations in action around the globe.

In this global market, we are much more than witnesses. Each of us is an architect of the world around us. Our everyday actions, even very personal ones such as what we choose to drink and eat, have an impact on the planet and its inhabitants. We are all interconnected. Thus we can choose to contribute to the world's problems, or to the development of some solutions. With our money, as little as we may have, we can vote for a world free of exploitation. Your vote can start with your morning coffee.

This book is thus about power: our power as consumers making daily choices to reorient the economy and shape the world we want to live in. Through the example of what is for many the first drink of the day, the following pages examine the issues surrounding the production and trading of coffee and the development of fair trade.

The first two chapters draw a broad picture of the current global context, addressing the issues surrounding the power of the market and its impact on democracy, and show how consumers hold some important tools for change in the emergence of a new, ethical consumer movement. Chapter 3 begins the story of coffee and presents its hidden social and environmental costs.

Using Mexico as an example, Chapter 4 describes the conventional coffee trade, tracing the coffee beans' journey from the tree, through the hands of several intermediaries in both the North and South, to its final destination as a cup of coffee. The fifth chapter presents an alternative route for coffee, via fair trade. This concept is concretely illustrated through the example of the Mexican peasant association, *Unión de Comunidades Indígenas de la Región del Istmo* (UCIRI). This organization was one of the first to embrace the fair-trade system and was also a pioneer in the production of organic and shade-grown coffee. Now hundreds of peasant organizations in Mexico and all over the world are taking part in the fair-trade and organic movement.

This growing producer-to-consumer movement is the subject of the final chapter, Chapter 6, which looks at notions of "sustainable" coffee such as "fair-trade," "organic" and "shade-grown," and then goes on to discuss the involvement of businesses and the role of certification. The book then concludes with a reflection on the consumer's power to hold up the stream of inequity.

Enjoy!

Notes

1. Pendergrast, Mark. *Uncommon Grounds: The History of Coffee and How It Transformed Our World.* New York: Basic Books, 1999. Also: Oxfam International. *Bitter Coffee: How the poor are paying for the slump in coffee prices.* Oxfam Policy Paper, Oxfam International, 2001.
2. www.business.com/directory/agriculture/philip_morris_companies/people/bible_geoffrey_c/
3. Oxfam International. op. cit.
4. Warwick, Hugh. "Trouble Brewing." *The Ecologist.* Vol. 31. No. 6. July-August 2001. 53.
5. *New York Times,* May 24, 2001.
6. Mander, Jerry, and Edward Goldsmith, ed. *The Case Against the Global Economy and for a turn toward the local.* San Francisco: Sierra Club Books,1996. Also: Salazar, Hilda, and Laura Carlsen. *The social and environmental impacts of NAFTA: Grassroots responses to economic integration.* Mexico: Red Mexicana de Acción Frente al Libre Comercio, 2001.

Chapter 1
The Global Context

Between the literal meaning of the word democracy, "rule by the people," and Abraham Lincoln's extended definition of "government of the people, for the people, and by the people,"[1] a wide range of interpretations are possible, depending on the class of people who rule.[2] Historians of Europe refer to the second half of the 15th century and the16th century as the *noblemen's democracy* and the 18th century as a *bourgeois democracy*.[3] Will our own era perhaps be remembered as a *corporate democracy?*

Corporations began their rise to become a dominant "social class" long ago. In 1886, a ruling by the US Supreme Court recognized corporations as "natural persons" under the American constitution. Court ruling by court ruling, legal rights were given to businesses as though they were citizens not only in the USA but also in other countries and within international law. The rights thus acquired by corporations throughout the world have increased their power in society, facilitating the establishment of mechanisms that help them reach their main objective: making profit.[4]

Today, corporations wield greater economic power than nations. This is especially true for the smallest countries. The coffee trade, for example, is dominated by a handful of multi-nationals, each having a turnover greater than the gross domestic product (GDP) of many coffee-producing nations: Nestlé's sales are more than 21 times the GDP of Nicaragua, while the operating revenues of Philip Morris exceed the GDP of Vietnam by almost three times.[5] And, as Maude Barlow and Tony Clarke report in *Global Showdown*, "Wal-Mart is bigger than 163 countries. Mitsubishi is larger than Indonesia. Ford is bigger than South Africa."[6]

States and corporations are speaking the same language, because profit and competitiveness have become the name of the game on the global market, and both wish to see the economy grow. We all take for granted that trade creates wealth. However, as we shall see, there are different ways of looking at what constitutes wealth.

The last 50 years have seen unprecedented economic growth and an explosion of financial flows. During this period, the sum of the world's gross domestic products has multiplied by more than six times in real terms, while average per-capita GDP has grown by almost three times.[7] Every day, over $1.5 trillion is exchanged in the world's currency markets, and nearly a fifth of the goods and services created each year are traded internationally.[8] For policymakers and businesses that believe in free trade, these numbers are an expression of "progress." But for whom?

Inequalities between rich and poor—people and nations—are increasing around the globe. Even such a staunch proponent of neo-liberal trade policies as *The Economist* acknowledges that the distribution of income is becoming more unequal.[9] As reported by the United Nations Development Programme (UNDP), the countries of the OECD (Organization for Economic Cooperation and Development), which represent only 19 percent of the world's population, account for 71 percent of global trade in goods and services and 58 percent of foreign direct investment. Although globally GDP has increased, in over 80 countries the average per-capita income is lower than a decade ago. Meanwhile, the assets of the planet's three richest men exceed the combined GDP of the 43 least developed countries and their 600 million people.[10]

The UNDP also highlights a recent surge of mergers and acquisitions, which concentrate industrial power in the hands of giant corporations, eroding competition. In 1998, the top 10 companies in pesticides controlled 85 percent of a $31 billion global market—and the top 10 in telecommunications, 86 percent of a $262 billion market.[11]

Adam Smith is celebrated as the father of free trade, but we would do well to remember his observation that "People of the same trade seldom meet together... but the conversation ends in a conspiracy against the publick, or in some contrivance to raise prices."[12] Smith predicted that market forces would act in favour of "natural progress," but only if the market were free from the control of a minority. Today, businesses are uniting into powerful lobby groups within the various Chambers of Commerce as well as within industrial groups such as the Business Council on National Issues (BCNI) in Canada, the European-American Business Council (EABC) and the European Round Table of Industrialists (ERT), to mention but a few. They have built intimate relationships with trade bureaucrats and governments all over the world.[13] They are pushing economic "growth" as an agenda that will bring benefits for everybody.

The way that growth and wealth are measured, however, pays little heed to the actual wellbeing of people, nor does it take future generations into account. The disappearance of species, contamination of water, the exploitation of workers and other ecological and social problems resulting from the intensification of production do not appear as costs on the balance sheet of businesses. Rather, they are considered as externalities, the costs of which are usually assumed by society as a whole—especially where environmental and social regulations are weak. On the other hand, the profits of the exploitation of the common good are privatized. Although it might have taken 200 or 2000 years for a forest to grow, when its wood is sold, profits go to the company that cut and processed it rather than to all those who are losing the forest. The production and trade of coffee provides another good example, as we will see in the later chapters.

The vast majority of economists, policymakers and members of the public consider per-capita GDP as the main indicator of economic health and progress. Our common wellbeing is thus summarized in a simple arithmetical calculation: a country's GDP is the value of domestic consumption, plus the value of business investments, plus the value of government spending, and the value of net exports (exports minus imports).[14] Valuable goods and services such as home childcare, clean water and home-grown food are not considered. Also, no allowance is made for the negative effects of economic activity. So $2 million spent on education contributes the same to the economy as $2 million spent on coffins. The construction of prisons and increased numbers of road accidents are also seen as contributions to the economy.

In this scheme, unless something has market value, it has no economic value at all. And if it has economic value, scant attention is paid to it in the political decision-making process. How would you measure the value of clean air, the care of a mother for her child, or simply happiness? Quantity is easier to quantify than quality.

Compare the situations of two people. The first is a small coffee farmer in Guatemala, living on his own land, and self-sufficient in food and accommodation. He has almost no money. The second lives in Mexico near the US border. She works in a sweatshop sewing shirts from 8am to 6pm six days a week. She pays rent and buys her food. Three times more money passes through her hands than through those of the coffee farmer. Is she happier? We cannot say for certain, even if few of us would choose her lot over that of the self-sufficient farmer. But our system of economic accounting implicitly considers that having more money is better.

The small farmer is too self-sufficient to contribute to economic growth. Little of his daily work has market value and thus is not reflected in the GDP. The sweatshop worker is seen as doing much more for the economy. She is making it grow. This kind of economic analysis motivates policymakers to stimulate exports rather than the meeting of local needs. The assumption is that the population will be better off with a greater income and the country with a greater GDP. But as the above example suggests, this is perhaps not so obvious.

Not only does GDP fail to calculate the real value of the world around us, but it also considers some negative goods and services positively. This becomes especially clear when we look at how environmental degradation contributes to economic growth. The clean water of a lake contributes nothing to economic growth, but cleaning it up if it were polluted would contribute. Air contamination leads to increased spending on health care, thereby contributing to the economy. Under this logic, it is better for the economy to respond to problems created by new technologies than to prevent them from happening. Who profits when new technologies are developed? Usually the private sector. Most often, the cost of remediation is borne by citizens, through their governments, rather than by the industries that create the pollution.

Many problems that have arisen from human disregard for nature can be neither evaluated nor repaired. This is the case for vanishing species, global warming and the destruction of indigenous cultures. None of these are deducted from GDP. As a result, an unprecedented, uncalculated and incalculable ecological and social debt is being created. One that the World Bank is not accounting for.

ECONOMIC GROWTH RULES SUPREME

The objective of economic growth at all costs through free trade has now become an end in itself rather than a means by which to achieve the wellbeing of people. It is eroding the State's traditional role of protecting its citizens and the environment. The emerging "sovereignty" of the "privately controlled" market is undoubtedly coming about with the support of the dominant States. The leaders of the world are accelerating the process of globalization by concluding international free-trade agreements that transform their own ability to intervene in the economy.

The concept of self-governance and its connection to distinct nation-State territorial boundaries is being redefined in the context of the increasing interdependence between nations.[15] A State used to be seen as a political body possessing sovereignty in its territory and over its inhabitants.[16] Today economic specialization among national economies combined with new international law restricts the capacity of national governments to be self-reliant, to choose their own economic system, or even to manipulate their domestic economies for social or environmental purposes.[17] States are further undermining their own autonomy as policymakers in the quest for global competitiveness and the race for productivity and profitability.[18] National sovereignty has thus become relative, with states wielding less and less supreme authority within their borders. Frontiers are becoming increasingly porous for goods and services, but not for individuals (with the exception of the European Union, for citizens of its member countries).

States today have become the mouthpieces of multinational corporations, facilitating their race for profit through "trade missions" and free-trade negotiations. This was obvious in Seattle at the World Trade Organization (WTO) Millennium Round in 1999 and in Québec City in 2001 at the Free Trade Agreement of the Americas (FTAA) meeting. At the first press conference organized by the Canadian government in Seattle, the only list of contacts given to the media was of business organizations and government representatives.[19] This makes it easy for journalists to get the opinion of the corporate sector. No contacts were given for organizations defending human rights, social justice or the environment. In Québec City, although a wall was built to keep citizens out of the enclave in which delegates were negotiating, corporations were welcomed in. Private enterprises such as Bombardier (an aerospace firm also involved in defence services) and Alcan (an aluminum company) were given access to representatives of governments from the entire "hemisphere" by sponsoring breakfasts or cocktail receptions at costs ranging from CDN $50,000 to $1.5 million.[20] Meanwhile, 60,000 citizens from all walks of life who wished to voice their opinions on the FTAA project were kept outside the wall.

MENTAL COLONIALISM

In today's global economy—just as during the imperial peri-od— global dominance remains a goal, but is apparently to be achieved through marketing rather than military strategy. Nowadays brand names, more than flags, symbolize the con-quests of the richest countries.[21] Multinational corporations move their operations from place to place, wherever conditions are most profitable.

Driven by the interests of these big corporations, citizens are to be conquered, but this time as consumers, using adver-tising. Our mental space is colonized with the help of powerful marketing strategies closely meshed with popular culture. The US movie industry is a highly effective vehicle for spreading the seeds of consumer culture across the globe and making people crave American products. Many of us have come to believe that we are, not what we eat, but what we consume.[22]

International treaties such as the North American Free Trade Agreement (NAFTA) and the World Trade Organization (WTO) further the power of corporations over States. The secretive manner in which trade negotiations are conducted keeps citizens—and even most elected representatives—far away from the process. These agreements provide for binding arbitration between states in a manner that puts trade before all other concerns. The WTO agreements include no minimum standards to protect the environment, human and labour rights, or cultural diversity. Such is their reach that they place limits on the power of governments to legislate in the areas of culture, health, education, environment, agriculture and natu-ral resources, to name but a few.[23] Renato Ruggiero, former Director of the WTO, makes the aim quite clear: "We are no longer writing the rules of interaction among separate national economies. We are writing the constitution of a single global economy."[24] The global market has become the new emperor of us all.

With this global constitution, decisions affecting millions of people are being made, not by national governments, and far less often by local institutions, but by agencies outside their national borders. Power has been transferred to unelected international bodies, making it almost impossible for ordinary citizens to affect decisions directly. The decisions of WTO trade bureaucrats in Geneva affect the lives of people all over the world.

The Agreement on Trade-Related Intellectual Property Rights (TRIP) within the WTO is only one example among many. This agreement permits corporations to establish property rights over traditional seeds and medicinal plants. These are new rights, allowing private corporations to patent life, overturning the long-held community-based rights of small farmers and wresting control from local communities over products and processes derived from traditional methods.[25]

Some regional trade agreements go even further than the WTO in disempowering citizens and their elected representatives and exposing them to the nefarious effects of the antisocial behaviour of corporations. Chapter 11 of NAFTA allows foreign investors to sue governments for current and anticipated loss of profit.[26] They can challenge national regulations that directly limit their sales. In 1997 the US company Ethyl Corporation sued the Canadian government for $251 million for prohibiting the import of one of its products, the gasoline additive MMT. This additive had already been banned in many countries because of the dangers it poses to human health and the environment. Realizing that it would lose the case, the Canadian government settled out of court. Not only did Canada remove its ban of MMT but Ethyl Corporation was paid $13 million in compensation, with Canadian taxpayers footing the bill. This is only one example of the pernicious effects of NAFTA on people and the environment; many others could be cited.[27]

The next chapter looks at how emerging social movements

are trying to oppose to the free-trade paradigm and propose alternatives. They are striving to rebuild democracy, redefining the rights and responsibilities of businesses and consumers in order to develop a sustainable trading system.

Notes

1. Lincoln, Abraham. November 19, 1863. *The Collected Works of Abraham Lincoln,* Vol. VII, edited by Roy P. Basler. showcase.netins.net/web/creative/lincoln/speeches/gettysburg.htm

2. Boudansky, Daniel. *The Legitimacy of International Governance: A Coming Challenge for International Environmental Law.* American Journal of International Law. Vol. 93, No. 3. (July, 1999). Also: Osmańczyk, Edmund Jan. *Encyclopedia of the United Nations and International Agreements.* Second Edition. (New York, Philadelphia and London: Taylor and Francis, 1990), 219. Also: *A Dictionary of International Law and Diplomacy.* (New York: Dobbs Ferry and Phonix Press Inc. 1973). *Webster's Encyclopedic Unabridged Dictionary of the English Language.* (New York: Gramercy Books 1989).

3. Osmańczyk. op.cit.

4. Barlow, Maude, and Tony Clark. *Global Showdown: How the New Activists Are Fighting Global Corporate Rule.* Toronto: Stoddart, 2001. Also: Korten, David C. *The Post Corporate World: Life After Capitalism.* San Francisco: Kumarian Press and Berrett-Koehler Publishers, 1999. 174.

5. Philip Morris Annual Report 2000, Nestlé Annual Report 2000 Also: UNDP, op.cit.

6. Barlow and Clarke op. cit. 19.

7. Johnson, Pierre-Marc, and Karel Mayrand. *Beyond Trade: The Case for a Broadened International Governance Agenda.* Montréal: Institute for Research on Public Policy, June 2000.

8. United Nations Development Programme. *Human Development Report 1999.* London: Oxford University Press, 1999. 1.

9. "Winners and Losers," *The Economist,* April 26, 2001.

10. UNDP. op. cit. 3.

11. Ibid.

12. Smith, Adam. *An Inquiry into the Nature and Causes of the Wealth of Nations.* Oxford and New York: Oxford University Press, 1993.

13. Barlow and Clarke. op.cit. Also: Korten op.cit. Also: Corporate Europe Observatory. *Europe, Inc.: Dangerous liaisons between EU institutions and industry.* Amsterdam: Corporate Europe Observatory, 1997.

14. Daly, Herman E., and B. Coob Jr. *For the Common Good: Redirecting the economy toward community, the environment, and a sustainable future.* Boston: Beacon Press, 1994.

15. McGrew, Antony. *The Transformation of Democracy?* Cambridge: Polity Press, 1997.

16. Canadian International Development Agency (CIDA). *Mini-dictionary of International Development.* Ottawa: Supply and Services Canada, 1990. 92.

17. Dyer, Gwynne. *Globalization of the Nation-State: Behind the Headlines.* Ottawa: Canadian Institute of International Affairs. (1996). 1-15.

18. Cerny, Philip G. *Globalization and the Erosion of Democracy.* European Journal of Political Research (Dordrecht). Vol. 36. (1999). 5.

19. I attended the Canadian Press Conference held on November 29, 1999 at the Mayflower Park Hotel in Seattle.

20. *La Presse,* May 21, 2001.

21. For a good overview of this process of corporate acculturation and branding, see Klein, Naomi. *No Logo: Taking on the brand bullies.* Toronto: Vintage Canada. 2000.

22. See the excellent work of Adbusters Media Foundation: www.adbusters.org.

23. Shrybman, Steven. *The World Trade Organization: A Citizen's Guide.* Ottawa: The Canadian Centre for Policy Alternatives, and Toronto: James Lorimer & Company, 1999.

24. UNCTAD. UNCTAD and WTO: A Common Goal in a Global Economy. Press Release. www.unctad.org/en/special/tb43pr05.htm.

25. Khor, Martin, "Global Economy and the Third World" in *The Case Against the Global Economy.* Sierra Club Books, San Francisco, 1996 Also: Shrybman. op.cit.

26. North American Free Trade Agreement Secretariat: www.nafta-sec-alena.org.

27. Petit, Martin and Martin Poirier, *Mondialisation et Environnement.* Institut de recherche et d'information socio-économique (IRIS), Montréal, April 2001.

Chapter 2
Rebuilding Democracy

As the structures of power are internationalized through more and stronger trade agreements, a growing sense of disempowerment is spreading throughout society.[1] The rumblings of anger are being felt across borders, across social classes, across the barriers of race, sex and age. Citizens are uniting and organizing to resist the overarching authority of the market, which is advanced to explain or justify almost every economic, political or social phenomenon. In many languages and in many ways people are saying no to the globalization of human and environmental exploitation. They are calling for the globalization of solidarity, for the building of an economy that is at the service of people, and not the opposite.

Even elected people, members of governments, are beginning to denounce the erosion of the democratic structures by international trade agreements. Unionists, human-rights activists, environmentalists, aboriginal people and women's groups have been walking side by side in Seattle, Prague, Washington, Nice and Québec City. These rallies are only one manifestation of a powerful undercurrent of revolution starting in people's heads and moving in the direction of daily action.

The United Nations estimated that in 1999 one person in five was involved in a civil-society organization.[2] The non-profit sector is growing at an unprecedented rate across the globe. Civil-society organizations are assuming responsibilities that have been abandoned by governments. Generally, they are doing so without a corresponding allocation of the resources needed to achieve such broad tasks. Through these groups of people, citizens are working to alleviate poverty, protect the environment, and defend minority groups. They are attempting to mend a social fabric torn by neo-liberal policies.

Citizens are also building spontaneous movements at the local level, where municipalities are showing themselves incapable of adequately addressing the numerous challenges begotten by economic globalization. Ordinary citizens who have never been involved in activism are taking actions to resist the global juggernaut, the "Think Big" model imposed upon them by the need to feed the international markets.

On August 28, 2000 in Sainte-Croix-de-Lotbinière, a small, conservative agricultural village on the St. Lawrence River in Québec, Canada, 36 local residents of all ages staged a four-hour sit-in at the office of their provincial member of parliament, Jean-Guy Paré.[3] None of them had any experience of civil disobedience, but all felt the need to mobilize for the health of their community and the environment. The quality of the community's water, soil and air was threatened by the proliferation of large-scale hog farms. They had already gone through the official channels of representation by writing letters, sending petitions and attending municipal council meetings to make their voices heard, but felt their concerns were being ignored.

These were well-informed citizens, asking their elected representative pointed questions and telling him what they hoped for their village and for their province. One of the leaders, Gildor Michaud, said: "When we elected you, it was not to make us competitive on the world market. We elected you to manage our everyday collective problems... but not under such conditions." A young mother holding her child added with emotion: "We voted for the health of our children, for a blue-print for society, for happiness, not for the destruction of our environment to benefit a few people who are making a lot of money selling their pigs to Japan. We want to be counted."

This is only one example among many across the world. As reflection turns into action, thousands of similar mobilizations of citizens are gathering pace around the world—often far from the media's gaze. In Paris, Amsterdam and Madrid people are squatting in unoccupied buildings. In Brazil landless people are reclaiming the land. In India villagers are organizing to counter genetically modified crops and the patenting of life.

As small as each of these gestures might appear taken individually, each is an important step in rebuilding democracy—from the bottom up. People have begun to question the prevailing economic system. The challenge will be to create a different one.

WHEN BUYING BECOMES VOTING

People are beginning to realize the power of their money, however little they might have. While in the dominant discourse citizens are seen as merely consumers, some consumers are now reclaiming their citizens' "rights" and responsibilities by putting their money where their values are. Every day, people are making personal choices that contribute to the construction of a responsible economy. Fair-trade, organic and other eco-friendly products are finding room in an increasing number of stores. Ethical and environmental investment funds have expanded to the point that Wall Street analysts are taking this trend seriously.[4] Investors are weighing the environmental and social-justice performance of the companies they invest in.[5] An increasing number of businesses have adopted codes of conduct. Ethical options are becoming available because people are asking for them, and because civil-society organizations have helped by creating a movement.

Responsible businesses are multiplying, thus moving sustainability from the realm of theory to that of practice. But although it is encouraging to see companies making voluntary efforts, government intervention is needed to develop mechanisms to ensure that real environmental and social costs are factored into management practices. Under current free-trade conditions, low environmental and social standards are comparative advantages, thus creating pressure on all countries to lower their standards. As long as environmental and social costs are not reflected in the prices paid by consumers, sustainable products will remain at a disadvantage compared to conventional products.

In Montréal, for example, a kilogram of bananas produced in Ecuador with the help of chemical pesticides and fertilizers can be bought for CDN $0.77 (US$0.23 per lb.), while the same weight of local apples grown organically costs on average three times as much. If environmental and social costs were included in the price we pay, the situation would be reversed. The costs in terms of the health and welfare of workers and the community would be added to the price of the bananas, as would the costs of decontaminating water and soil in the growing areas. In a market where prices reflected all the costs of production, people would more naturally make sustainable consumer choices. In this case they would be likely to buy more local organic apples than conventionally produced bananas simply because they would be much cheaper.

The same logic would apply for other products: not only local organic food, but also recycled, fair-trade and small-business products. Market studies clearly indicate that, at comparable prices, consumers prefer to buy products with the least negative social and environmental impacts. Factoring in environmental and social costs would help to restructure the economy around sustainable modes of production and trade. Under such conditions, multinational corporations would find it difficult to compete.

This would be true free trade: current trade is highly subsidized.

Trade is directly subsidized by rich nations who unfairly flood world markets with cheap commodities, particularly food products, thereby putting small farmers in countries which cannot compete in the subsidy game out of business. Indirectly, trade is subsidized by workers who do not receive a fair wage or fair conditions for their work. By the artificially low prices of energy that do not reflect the costs of depletion of nonrenewable resources and the costs of pollution. By governments and local communities that bear the costs of cleaning up rivers and reestablishing ecosystems and the health costs resulting from a contaminated or damaged environment. And ultimately, trade is subsidized by future generations that will not be able to enjoy the diversity of species and culture that their ancestors took for granted, or expose their bare skin to the sun.

BRINGING ETHICS INTO THE EQUATION

As awareness of this artificial subsidy of trade grows, new definitions of commercial ethics, calling for a truly "new world order" are being articulated—even in spheres known for conservatism. Ethics has become a cutting-edge subject in the faculties of management in many institutions. At McGill University in Montréal, the undergraduate program includes a core course (The Social Context of Business) that awakens students to the less savoury aspects of current business practices. A new concentration stream is being instituted, developing students' understanding and orienting their skills towards work in noncorporate sectors. "McGill Business Watch" has become the most popular student club of the faculty, with more than 70 members monitoring the social and environmental practices of corporations and disseminating their findings via a growing internet newsgroup.

Large companies such as Nike and Walmart are being persuaded to improve some of their practices by new currents such as the "Natural Capitalism" propounded by Paul Hawken. This movement speaks to mainstream industries by defending a model which explores the lucrative opportunities for businesses in an era of increasing environmental restrictions.[6] Although regarded by some as too timid, Natural Capitalism represents a first positive step for some multinational corporations known for environmental and social practices that are among the worst.

Businesses are coming to realize the power of consumers. A recent management guide by Patricia B. Seybold, *The Customer Revolution*, provides a striking example of this trend. She argues that the relationships built by a company with its customers are now more important than all the capital stored in its buildings and bank accounts. As Seybold puts it, "every industry is under siege by its customers."[7] (...) "Companies are valued based on their future earning potential. Where do companies' earnings come from? From consumers. To increase your earning potential, you need to focus on winning and retaining profitable consumers whose needs you're serving. It's as simple as that."[8]

A side-effect of this discourse can be seen in the way that some companies are donning the cloak of social and environmental responsibility to make themselves look good. In 1999, for example, the cigarette, food and coffee giant Philip Morris gave $60 million to charity and spent a further $108 million on advertisements to make sure the world knew about its generosity.[9]

In general, though, a lack of information about the environmental and social practices of corporations makes it difficult for consumers to make judicious choices. Although we may recognize some "responsible" certification seals, such as "organic" and "fair trade," most of the products that surround us give little clue about the companies we are funding with our everyday purchases. In the case of coffee for example, someone might choose the brand Nabob, deducing from the package that it is produced by a small Canadian company, whereas in fact it belongs to the tobacco giant, Philip Morris (see p. 58 for more details).[10]

A clear identification of ethical products is necessary. Civil-society organizations at the Environmental Forum of the 2001 Peoples Summit in Québec City proposed the establishment of national and international labelling systems that would compel companies to provide independently monitored social and environmental information about their products.[11] This would help to give a market value to social and environmental criteria and encourage the creation of mechanisms to include social and environmental costs in the price of what we buy. The obligation to provide this kind of information on labels would create pressure on companies to show themselves as more environmentally and socially responsible.

To create and enforce such a system would require serious commitment from governments around the world. Current agreements within the World Trade Organization (WTO) are moving in the opposite direction. Indeed, under agreements currently being studied, environmental and social regulatory standards are considered, *prima facie*, Technical Barriers to Trade (TBT).[12] Discrimination between products on the basis of *where* they are produced and distinguishing between products based on *how* they are made are prohibited. Europe and Mexico have already won a dispute with the USA in the "Tuna-Dolphin" case: under the WTO ruling, the USA was obliged to amend its Marine Mammal Protection Act, thus modifying its "dolphin-safe" law which required safe fishing practices. "Dolphin-safe" certification standards were thereby weakened.[13] As we will see in a later chapter, sustainable-coffee initiatives are not immune from WTO regulation.

Sustainability should be a requirement for all trade, and not merely a means for well-off, educated consumers to feel good about themselves. But to achieve this, much work needs to be done at the political level: government standards would have to be strengthened internationally so that low environmental and labour regulations cease to be comparative advantages that only benefit multinational corporations.

If countries are able to agree on effective global mechanisms to facilitate commerce, why are they not capable of doing so with regard to environmental protection and social justice? Conventions and multilateral agreements to address humanitarian and ecological issues are numerous, but none has the binding power of trade agreements such as NAFTA or the WTO.[14] Otherwise, the USA would not have been able to abandon the Kyoto Protocol and other agreements regarding the arms trade and human rights.

For the time being there are no global agreements to ensure that trade is sustainable. However, some enlightened producers, traders and consumer organizations are slowly opening a breach in an economic system that has been built over time on the exploitation of people and the environment. They are using the market as a vehicle for environmental and social justice. To give force to the emerging ethical-trade movement, it helps to understand the workings of the system. This brings us to the "coffee machine."

Notes

1. McGrew, op. cit.
2. United Nations Development Programme (UNDP). *Human Development Report 2000.* London: Oxford University Press, 2000.
3. National Film Board of Canada. Shoots from Hugo Latulippe filmed on August 28, 2000 at Ste-Croix-de-Lotbinière, in preparation for the documentary "Bacon" released in September 2001.
4. Sauvé, Mathieu-Robert. "Les bonnes actions." *L'Actualité (Montréal).* Vol. 26, No. 2 (February 2001), 66.
5. For more information on ethical investments: www.socialinvestment.ca
6. Natural Capitalism web page: www.naturalcapitalism.org. Also: Hawken, Paul. *The Ecology of Commerce: A Declaration of Sustainability.* Harper Business: New York, 1994. xiv
7. Seybold, Patricia B. *The Customer Revolution: How to thrive when customers are in control.* New York: Crown Business, 2001. xvi.
8. Ibid. xv.
9. Adbusters. March/April 2001. No. 34. 38.
10. Philip Morris web page: www.philipmorris.com.
11. Second People's Summit. "Déclaration du Forum Environnement." Montréal: Regroupement Québécois des Groupes Écologistes, April 18, 2001.
12. Shrybman. op. cit. 11.
13. Wallach, Lori, and Michelle Sforza. *Whose Trade Organization?* Washington, D.C.: Public Citizen, 1999. 22-29.
14. Johnson and Mayrand. op. cit.

Chapter 3
Coffee and its Hidden Costs

Coffee is part of the everyday lives of billions of people all over the world. North Americans consume more than 4 kg (9 lb.) of the black drink per capita per year, which averages out to about two cups per day for every man, woman and child.[1] In 70 Southern countries, coffee is also the livelihood of 20 million workers of all ages who pick over 6 million tonnes of beans annually.[2] The International Coffee Organization has estimated that approximately 11 million hectares of the world's farmland is dedicated to coffee cultivation—an area roughly the size of the State of Ohio, or of Switzerland, Belgium and the Netherlands combined.[3]

Coffee is one of the most widely traded products on the international market and is the top foreign-currency earner for many nations.[4] Cultivated almost exclusively in developing nations, it represents an important cash crop needed for debt repayment. For countries such as Uganda, Burundi and Rwanda, coffee represents up to 80 percent of total exports.[5] Latin American countries like Colombia, Guatemala and Nicaragua also depend on coffee exports, although to a lesser extent: it represents around 20 percent of their export earnings.[6] Price fluctuations on the commodity exchanges of New York or London thus have a tremendous impact, especially on the less diversified economies.

THE HISTORY OF COFFEE

The coffee tree is indigenous to Ethiopia and its fruit is said to have first been harvested in the province of Kaffa in the mid-12th century.[7] Traders brought coffee to the Middle East, from where it began to spread outwards in the 15th century, penetrating every corner of Europe over the next two hundred years. Coffee houses became popular meeting places where intellectual and philosophical questions were debated.[8]

During the 18th and 19th centuries, the spread of coffee cultivation and trade was rooted in colonialism. Coffee had become a highly prized commodity in Europe and could be cultivated in many tropical areas. The Dutch were the first to introduce the crop to their colony in what is now Indonesia, followed by the British and the French in the Caribbean and the Portuguese in Brazil. Natives were enslaved to work in the coffee plantations, and slaves were brought from Africa.[9]

The practices of colonialism and slavery persisted in many coffee-growing areas, and their echoes are still felt today: poor labour practices and dependency on industrialized countries remain a dominant feature of coffee production and trade. During the period of decolonization, coffee was put forward as a miracle crop that would allow developing countries to achieve economic growth.[10] This promise was never fulfilled. Today, as always, prices fall as more and more coffee is brought onto the market, because demand never grows at the same rate. A recent example has been the vast expansion of coffee production in Vietnam, precipitating a major collapse in world coffee prices. Only when a natural disaster strikes a major coffee-producing area, such as the severe frosts in Brazil in 1994, does the price of coffee rise.

COFFEE IN MEXICO

Coffee production in Mexico dates back to 1795. Although at first the bulk of the coffee crop was sold on the domestic market, production intensified rapidly to meet increasing international demand.[11] Small locally owned farms were quickly replaced by large plantations financed primarily by foreign capital, mostly German, but also American and British.[12] As historian Armando Bartra reports, "plantations functioned as economic enclaves, trying to present a modern image, but imposing slave-like conditions on workers."[13] Living conditions for workers and their families were miserable: they were kept in a situation of almost complete dependence on the landowners, receiving barely enough income to survive.

The agrarian revolution that swept through Mexico during the 1930s improved this situation somewhat by giving peasants the chance to own land. However, the big coffee producers were able to hold on to the most fertile land, as well as their factories and commercial contacts, and have maintained this advantageous position to the present day. Although they represent only 8 percent of producers, large landowners amass more than 90 percent of the profits from the sales of unroasted Mexican coffee.[14]

In fact, despite legislation that theoretically favours the poorest Mexican farmers, the concentration of land in the hands of the wealthy is progressively intensifying, arguably as the result of global economic transformations. The North American Free Trade Agreement (NAFTA) forced Mexico to transform its traditional community-based land system to facilitate privatization.[15]

NAFTA promised huge benefits for Mexico. In agricultural trade, Mexico was supposed to be able to buy American cereals at cheaper prices, while Mexican fruits and vegetables were supposed to have easier access to the lucrative Northern markets. With this in mind, the Mexican government under President Carlos Salinas increased agricultural aid for export crops and reduced its support for subsistence crops such as corn and beans. Furthermore, a public-sector organization responsible for buying a large part of the harvest, the *Compañía Nacional de Subsistencias Populares* (CNSP), was dismantled. This caused a drop in the production of basic staple crops and an indiscriminate increase in rice, bean and other grain imports. For many small Mexican producers, farming basic grains was no longer feasible and they had no other option but to sell their land and look for jobs in overpopulated cities or immigrate illegally to the United States.

This resulted in a drop in cereal production (20 percent in 1996 alone) and the migration of thousands of Mexican farmers to the already overpopulated towns and cities.[16]

THE ENVIRONMENTAL COST OF COFFEE

Like most agricultural sectors, coffee production has been intensified under the "green revolution." During the 1970s the modernization of agriculture led to the development of high-yielding varieties of coffee which did not need to be grown under the forest canopy. Production density could thus increase from 1,100-1,500 to 4,000-7,000 trees per hectare. Intensive "monocropping" plantations came to replace the diverse shade-grown ecosystems common in some traditional coffee plantations. Colombia and Costa Rica have led the way in modernizing coffee plantations. In Colombia, it has been estimated that 68 percent of coffee is grown in closely-packed rows under full sun, while in Costa Rica this method accounts for 40 percent of production.[17]

In many parts of the world this intensification has led not only to increased coffee production but also to serious environmental problems. These issues are increasingly being investigated by independent studies, such as those by the Smithsonian Migratory Bird Center.[18] Some of their findings follow.

Deforestation

Replacing shade-grown coffee plantations with intensive sun-resistant production has contributed to tropical deforestation.[19] Mountain forests are being cut down at an alarming rate and replaced by monocropping coffee plantations. Such forests play an important ecological role by protecting atmospheric dynamics, water quality, and wildlife species.[20]

Lost biodiversity

Deforestation and monocropping leads to major losses of habitats and reductions in the biodiversity of insects, animals and plants.[21] For example, studies done in Mexico and Colombia by the Smithsonian Migratory Bird Center indicate there are over 90 percent fewer bird species in sun-grown plantations than in shade-coffee plantations.[22]

Agrochemical pollution

Compared with traditional shade-coffee systems, sun cultivation is dependent upon increased use of chemical pesticides and fertilizers.[23] Contamination has been documented in a number of intensive coffee-production areas from Jamaica to Indonesia.[24] Some of the chemicals being used in intensive coffee production have been banned in industrial countries because of their possible carcinogenicity or long-term persistence in the environment. The use of agrochemicals directly affects the health of farmers and rural people, as well as the quality of soil and water and its inhabitants.

Soil erosion

Monocropping of coffee can cause significant deterioration in soil quality and increased erosion. Mountainous areas are particularly fragile environments. It has been documented that in high-rainfall areas, nearly three times more soil nitrogen is lost in unshaded than in shade plantations.[25]

Genetically modified coffee

Unknown environmental threats are hanging over coffee ecosystems. Genetically modified coffee varieties have been patented by the company Integrated Coffee Technologies Inc. (ICTI).[26] This Hawaii-based firm has developed caffeine-free coffee plants, as well as a new variety with a special ripening process which makes all the coffee berries ripen at the same time, reducing the amount of labour needed for the harvest. The natural ripening process is "switched off" until the crop is sprayed with ethylene.[27] Not only does this new variety of coffee increase farmers' dependency on chemicals, but, as with other genetically modified organisms, the long-term effects on people and the environment remain unknown. Once let loose in the environment, genetically modified organisms cannot be put back into a bottle. The planet becomes an uncontrolled global laboratory.

Overall, the environmental problems generated by coffee production and trade remain numerous and complex. Industrial techniques used to increase yield and farmers' revenues have benefited some coffee-growing countries, but most of the benefits have accrued to those able to afford the new technologies, that is, those that are already better off. On the other hand, further environmental degradation has contributed to long-term collective impoverishment. Past experience makes abundantly clear the need to develop integrated solutions that would balance social and environmental sustainability in a holistic manner.

The free-trade markets of today may be effective at setting prices, but they are totally incapable of recognizing the true production costs of what we buy.[28] If these hidden social and environmental costs were included in the price consumers paid for their morning coffee, the demand for organic and fair-trade brands would skyrocket, because they would be considerably cheaper than conventionally produced coffee. The result would be an improvement in the situation of coffee growers, and greater respect for the environment.

BREW FOR THE BIRDS

On a beautiful sunny morning, while you enjoy a leisurely breakfast on the balcony, the connection between the coffee you are sipping and the singing of the birds you can probably hear around you may not be apparent. It may surprise you to learn that conventional coffee production is decimating some of our local bird species, as has been discovered by researchers at the Smithsonian Migratory Bird Center in Washington.

The warblers, thrushes, finches and flycatchers we tend to take for granted leave their North American breeding grounds in the fall to spend the winter in the warmer climes of Central America. Traditional coffee plantations provide an ideal wintering ground for these migrant birds: the coffee plants grow in the shade, surrounded by a wide variety of other trees and plants. Forty to fifty species of trees can be found within a few hectares of coffee plantation and, not surprisingly, this rich and biologically diverse habitat appeals to other creatures, such as insects, snakes, bats, squirrels and even howler monkeys.

But, like the tropical rainforests, this habitat is disappearing. More and more traditional coffee plantations are being turned over to more intensive "sun-coffee" production, with up to 7,000 coffee trees crammed into one hectare (2,800 trees per acre).

This type of cultivation requires chemical fertilizers and pesticides that can be damaging to the environment and to the health of the plantation workers. The traditionally rich and diverse habitats of mixed tree and plant vegetation are torn out to increase space available for coffee trees, with the result that the animals that live there are suddenly made homeless. Although other factors are involved, such as local forest fragmentation and the destruction of Northern woodlands, ornithologists are certain that the widespread trend towards intensive coffee production across Central America and the Caribbean is implicated in the significant decline in the population of species such as the Cape May warbler, the Tennessee warbler and the Baltimore Oriole.

Russ Greenberg and colleagues at the Smithsonian Institute are so convinced of this coffee-conservation connection that they organized the first Sustainable Coffee Congress in Washington D.C. in September 1996. Participants failed to agree over the solutions to this growing problem, but all were certain of the power of the consumer over the coffee markets. By demanding shade-grown, fairly traded, organic coffee we can help to ensure the survival of the small traditional coffee plantations, the people who work on them, and the birds that shelter there.

Jackie Kirk

Notes

1. Statistics Canada #32-229-XPB. *Food consumption in Canada,* Part 1, Department of Industry, June 1999, Ottawa.

2. Rice, Paul D., and Jennifer McLean. *Sustainable Coffee at the Crossroads.* Washington, D.C.: Consumer's Choice Council, October 15, 1999. 21.

3. Rice and McLean. op. cit. 12.

4. United Nations Conference on Trade and Development, www.unctad.com

5. Dicum, Greg, and Nina Luttinger. *The Coffee Book: Anatomy of an industry from crop to the last drop.* New York: The New Press, 1999. 100.

6. Ibid.

7. Wrigley, Gordon. *Coffee,* New York: Longman Scientific & Technical, 1988.

8. Dicum and Luttinger. op. cit.

9. Ibid., 26.

10. Ibid., 75.

11. Museo Nacional de Culturas Populares. *La Vida en un Sorbo.* Exhibition Mexico City. May 1996-February 1997.

12. Bartra, Armando. *El México Bárbaro: Plantaciones Y Monterías Del Sureste Durante El Porfiriato.* Mexico City: El Atajo Ediciónes, 1996.

13. Ibid.

14. Museo National de Culturas Populares. op. cit.

15. Diebel, Linda. "Mexicans Paying Big Price for NAFTA." *Toronto Star.* April 15, 2001.

16. Lehman, Karen. "Au Mexique, les fausses promesses de l'Alena." *Le monde diplomatique.* November 1996, 26.

17. Rice, Robert A., and Justin R. Ward. *Coffee, Conservation, and Commerce in the Western Hemisphere.* Washington, D.C.: Smithsonian Migratory Bird Center, 1996. Also: Pendergrast. op. cit. 400.

18. See bibliography for full list.

19. Pendergrast op. cit. Also: Perfecto, I., and J. Vandermeer. "Microclimatic changes and the indirect loss of ant diversity in a tropical agroecosystem." *Oecologia* Vol.108 (November 1996): 577-582. Also: Perfecto, I; Vandermeer, J.; Hanson, P. and Cartin, V. "Arthropod biodiversity loss and the transformation of tropical agro-ecosystem." *Biodiversity and Conservation*, Vol. 6, July 7, 1997, 935-945. Also: Perfecto and Vandermeer. op. cit. 1996

20. Rice and Ward. op. cit.

21. Perfecto, Vandermeer, Hanson, and Cartin. op. cit. Also: Greenberg, Russel, Peter Bichier, Andrea Angon Cruz, and Robert Reitsma. "Bird Populations in Shade and Sun Coffee Plantations in Central Guatemala." *Conservation Biology.* Vol. 11 (April 1997): 448-459. Also: Greenberg, Russel. "Birds in the Tropics, The Coffee Connection." *Birding* (Washington, D.C.). December 1996: 472-481.

22. Rice and Ward. op. cit.

23. Robins. Robert and Abbot. op. cit. Also: Lumbanraja, J., T. Syam,. H. Nishide, A. K. Mahi, M. Utomo, and M. Kimura. "Deterioration of Soil Fertility by Land Use Changes in South Sumatra, Indonesia: from 1970-1990." *Hydrological Processes.* October-November 1998: 2003-2013.

24. Ibid.

25. Rice and Ward. op.cit.

26. Integrated Coffee Technologies Inc. (ICTI): www.integratedcoffee.com.

27. Kirby, Alex. "GM coffee threatens farmers." *BBC News Online.* Thursday, May 17, 2001.

28. Hawken, Paul. *The Ecology of Commerce: A declaration for sustainability.* New York: HarperBusiness, 1993. 133.

Chapter 4
The Conventional Coffee Route

The situation of coffee growers varies from one country to another with many factors, including State involvement in regulating labour and agricultural practices and in supporting social programs in rural areas. Costa Rica, for example, considered one of the most advanced developing countries in terms of human development, provides better infrastructure and social services to its coffee growers than Ethiopia, where environmental degradation and poverty are much more prevalent for the population in general.[1] Another example is Colombia, where the Colombian Coffee Federation (FNC) has a membership of over 500,000 coffee farmers having an average plantation size of less than two hectares. Collectively they have been successful in securing a price premium for Colombian coffee on the international market: the FNC's massive marketing campaign featuring "Juan Valdez," the "happy coffee farmer," has boosted the demand for Colombian coffee, helping to secure a higher standard of living for growers.[2] The Colombian example shows that coffee farmers' incomes can be raised, and that collective marketing of a quality product is a viable approach. However, Colombia is an exception in the coffee world, and its achievements might appear less glowing if the environmental impact of technical developments in the coffee plantations, discussed earlier, were taken into account.

Coffee beans follow a long and winding path, passing through the hands of many intermediaries before they reach our coffeepots. This chain varies from country to country because States use different mechanisms, from regulated auction systems in East African countries to a mixture of private and nationalized purchasing in Colombia. In general, however, the "coffee route" resembles the diagram opposite, inspired by the case of Mexico.

LINK 1: SMALL COFFEE PRODUCERS AND WORKERS

Roughly half of the world's coffee supply comes from small farms with less than five hectares of coffee trees.[3] Incomes tend to be low among families who run small coffee farms—most make an average annual cash income of between $600 and $1,200.[4] While small growers usually sell a kilogram of their coffee for between $0.33 and $1.50 ($0.15-$0.70 per lb.), by the time it reaches consumers it has acquired a price tag of between $8 and $30 (between $4 and $14 per lb.).[5]

Despite the variations in government services alluded to above, the situation of peasant farming families in the South is similar from one continent to another. Most are caught in the vicious cycle of poverty.[6] They have access to limited lands and limited resources. Because they are encouraged to specialize in production for export, their agriculture is not adequately diversified to meet all their own dietary requirements, nor is their income sufficient to buy foods that are no longer produced locally.[7]

Since peasants do not produce enough coffee to export directly, most have no choice but to sell their crop to local merchants (known as "coyotes" in Latin America) at low prices. Without sufficient funds to meet their needs from one harvest to the next, many peasants borrow money from these local intermediaries, who often represent the only possible source of finance in the village. Although governments may from time to time offer loan programs, these are most often oriented towards specific projects, such as the purchase of pesticides or

The Conventional Coffee Path
From coffee tree to cup

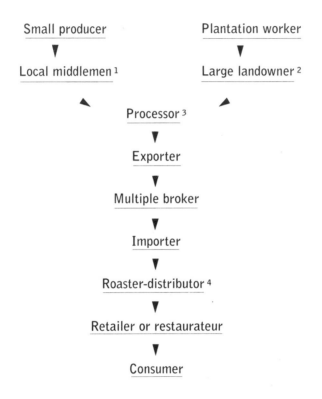

---

1. There can be more than one level of intermediary trader.
2. Large landowners most often have their own processing plants.
3. Coffee must be shelled and classified prior to export. Some coffee processors export directly, others are linked to multinational corporations in importing countries.
4. Typically, coffee companies roast, package and market their coffee.

the planting of certain export crops. The government does not lend money for the purchase of corn or beans when the food supply is exhausted or for medicine when a child falls ill. Under these circumstances, peasants turn to the coyote; in return for a loan, they agree to hand over their harvest at a very low price. Once in debt in this way, few peasants are able to break out of the cycle.

Farm workers are even more vulnerable than peasants. These men, women and children move from plantation to plantation where labour is abundant, salaries low and enforcement of labour and safety laws weak. Farm workers on coffee estates earn an average of only $2-3 per day.[8] During the harvesting season, migrant worker families move from one plantation to another, following the ripening of the beans, which depends on the climate and the altitude. They are usually paid according to the quantity of coffee they pick, with the result that even the youngest members of the family work long days. In Mexico, thousands of Guatemalans cross the border to work in coffee plantations. On some remote estates workers have to pay for their food and accommodation on site, which leaves very little money at the end of the day. The living conditions on most plantation sites are notoriously overcrowded, with men, women and children packed into crude barracks. Poor sanitary conditions, inadequate nutrition and daily exposure to agrochemicals take their toll on the health of those who grow our daily brew.[9]

In the coffee-production system, in Mexico and elsewhere, the benefits of production on what are usually the most fertile lands remain the privilege of large property owners who capitalize on greater land holdings, yields and production volumes.

Isolation
In Mexico, over 260,000 coffee growers farm at an altitude of between 600 and 1,500 metres (approx. 2,000 and 5,000 ft.), where lands are mountainous and susceptible to erosion.[10] The majority are indigenous people living in very remote regions. Many villages are not accessible by road, with the result that

the availability of services such as health care, education, and communication networks is severely limited.

For example, in the Istmo region, renowned for its coffee production, there is one doctor for every 2,780 inhabitants, compared with the national average of one for every 1,850 and the average of one for every 390 in industrialized countries.[11] Some villages are a two-day walk from the nearest medical centre. The inaccessibility of health care is particularly constraining in emergency situations.

Although primary-level education is available in most villages, teachers usually work at a second job to supplement their low salaries. The quality of education is therefore compromised by the teachers' frequent absences. Few village children go on to secondary school, because their parents cannot afford to send them away to the larger towns where secondary schools are usually located.

Isolation is one of the key reasons why free trade fails to deliver its promised benefits to small farmers. Their lack of market information, competitive markets and real economic choices all contribute to their exploitation, constituting a textbook example of "market failure."

Food insecurity

The population of the Istmo region faces a multitude of dietary deficiencies. According to Aurora and Gregoria de Anda, doctors in the region, malnutrition is a major problem in rural areas: "People eat a lot of tortillas and black beans here, but few vegetables. They generally have enough to eat, in terms of quantity, but not in terms of quality. Many lack necessary vitamins and minerals."[12] Dietary deficiencies make people vulnerable to diseases that would be easily prevented if they had a diversified diet and adequate sanitation. Malnutrition is believed to be one of the primary causes of the high infant-mortality rate in the area, reported by local doctors to be twice the national average.[13]

In the village of San José el Paraiso there are 13 places to buy soft drinks, yet only one which sporadically sells fresh fruits and vegetables. In May, when Mexican tomatoes invade Canadian and American supermarkets, they sell in San José for about the same price, approximately $1.80 per kg ($0.82 per lb.). Since Mexican wages are far lower than ours, tomatoes remain a luxury for these people. This is a good example of free trade at work. Why don't they grow their own tomatoes? Because tomato plants are fragile and do not always grow well in mountainous regions. People prefer to devote their time to growing corn, black beans and coffee.

Despite malnutrition among its population, Mexico exports nearly $4 billion worth of agricultural produce each year, mainly fruits and vegetables.[14] How is one to explain that those who work to ensure that Northern consumers enjoy year-round access to diverse and abundant foods themselves suffer from malnutrition? We can conclude that the rules of the international market fail to ensure the fair distribution of resources, with the result that the basic needs of many people are not met.

Coffee production

Coffee production demands intense work, great care, and ample time, especially for growers who use no chemical fertilizers or pesticides. Stakes are used for planting, machetes and axes for clearing, and picks and shovels for general work, but the most important tool remains the farmer's hands.

A coffee tree must grow for about four years before it gives any fruit. Specially selected grains are sprouted in a nursery. The soil must be prepared before saplings are transplanted. After about a year, trees must be pruned to direct their energy towards fruit production rather than plant growth. Coffee trees are frequently weeded to control the growth of other plants, which reduce the availability of soil nutrients for the coffee trees.

The harvest season is a period of intense activity. Entire communities are mobilized, women and children included. In big plantations, seasonal workers come from all across the country and even from Central America. It is crucial that the fruit be picked at just the right moment. If beans are picked too soon, the quality is inferior, but if left to ripen too long, the crop may be knocked off by the next heavy rainfall.

After picking, the fruit is "de-pulped." In the Istmo region, this is typically done using a small hand-mill. The husks are sifted out, leaving two coffee beans from each berry. The coffee beans are left to ferment for a few days, then washed and left to dry on a cement platform outdoors.

THE COFFEE TREE

There are two main coffee varieties, *Coffea arabica* and *C. robusta*. The Arabica tree is less productive than the Robusta, but its flavour is considered superior and consequently it accounts for about 70 percent of global coffee production. Certain coffee-tree species may reach heights of 15 metres (almost 50 ft.), but the Arabica trees grown in Mexico measure only 2 to 3 metres (6 ft. 6 in. to 10 ft.) The fruit is red or yellow when ripe, and the vast majority of the berries contain two seeds or coffee beans, positioned face to face. Depending upon the region, the species and the methods of cultivation, a coffee tree may produce for 20 to 30 years. Coffee is grown in both tropical and subtropical zones. Arabica trees grow best in a mild, mountainous climate where the temperature ranges between 18 and 24° C (64 and 75° F) and the seasons are well defined. Robusta trees produce fruit all year round, while Arabica trees provide a single annual harvest.

Source: Ferré, Felipe. *L'aventure du café*. Milan: Denoël, 1988.

Use of chemicals

Most coffee growers apply chemical fertilizers and pesticides. Colombia alone used nearly 400,000 tonnes of chemical fertilizer in 1994—approximately half a kilogram of chemicals for every kilogram of green coffee produced![15]

The application of chemicals tends to increase harvests and reduce workloads in the short term. However, in time a dependency is created because weeds and pests become resistant to pesticides, requiring the use of more powerful and dangerous chemicals. Production is also shifted from a labour-intensive to a capital-intensive system, favouring big farmers over small ones, and exacerbating already high levels of rural unemployment.

Several types of chemicals that have been banned in Northern countries on account of their extreme toxicity continue to be used in the South.[16] DDT, lindane and paraquat are top sellers in agrochemical stores in the Istmo region because of their low cost in comparison to less toxic alternatives.[17]

These poisons affect the health of local people and the environment to varying degrees, depending upon the toxicity of the product and the quantity applied. Despite the warnings printed on the containers, there is little knowledge of how to handle pesticides appropriately. Illiteracy rates are high, and the prescribed precautions are rarely followed. In rural areas, agrochemical products are often transported in open trucks: people, foodstuffs and all other products bound for a given destination are packed in alongside these dangerous chemicals. These conditions, combined with tropical temperatures, increase the risk of accidents. In homes, it is not uncommon to find pesticides stored unprotected in bedrooms or kitchens.

As for application, peasants rarely use any protective equipment, not even masks or gloves. Pesticides are prepared with water before application. This is often done next to a river whose water is used for drinking, bathing, washing clothes and cleaning animals.

LINK 2: THE LOCAL TRADER

Latin-American peasants use the name *coyote* for the intermediary traders to whom they sell their coffee. Coyotes are found at several levels of the coffee trade, from the lowest coyote who buys directly from farmers, to the top coyote who exports to international buyers. Their strategies, power and influence vary from one region to another, but generally their interests carry great weight, even in government, where they have strong allies.[18]

Coyotes are part of the local elite in Mexico. They act as

PESTICIDES

The effects of pesticides (insecticides, herbicides and others) on the environment and human health vary. Here are several side-effects which may be associated with pesticide use:

Environment
- Contamination of waterways and water tables (aquifers)
- Damage to soil microorganisms
- Exponential destruction of biodiversity (flora and fauna)
- Erosion
- Reproductive problems among livestock
- Eutrophication (overgrowth of algae) in rivers
- Persistence in the environment
- Air pollution
- Pesticide-resistant weeds and insects
- Contribution to the destruction of the ozone layer

Human health
- Headaches
- Digestive difficulties
- Eye irritations
- Respiratory problems
- Skin irritation
- Sterility
- Cancers
- Fatal poisonings

Sources: Shirley, A.*Basic Guide to Pesticides: Their Characteristics and Hazards*. Washington: Rachel Carson Council, Hemisphere Publishing Corporation, 1991. Also: Pesticide Action Network: www.pan.org.

bankers, often provide the local transportation system, and own the main general store. In some areas, this virtual monopoly allows them to control nearly all the economic activities of a village.

If the only vehicle in an area is owned by a coyote, he can control most of what enters or leaves the village. If coyotes own the only store in the village, they can control all the prices. The upshot is that peasants are frequently totally dependent on the coyotes, who buy their coffee, give them credit, sell them foodstuffs, and transport them or their products to larger centres of trade. The coyotes offer loans to peasants, but usually on the condition that farmers mortgage their coffee harvest at a very low price and/or repay the loans at extremely high rates of interest.

LINK 3: THE PROCESSOR
Coffee beans are subject to a final process before exportation. The fine skin which covers each bean must be removed with expensive machinery. Processors are often small entrepreneurs—also called coyotes by producers—although in some cases, processing is done in factories owned by multinational coffee corporations. The beans are then graded according to their shape, colour and density. Sophisticated machinery is used in this grading process. Finally, the beans, still green, are packed into 60 kg (132 lb.) sacks and sent to the exporter.

LINK 4: THE EXPORTER
The role of private exporters is to prepare a product that meets the very precise demands of the importer. They must make sure the right type of coffee is sent to the right place at the right time. Their goal, naturally, is the same as that of every intermediary: to buy coffee at the lowest price and resell it at the highest profit.

The best-quality coffee is exported, while lower grades are sold on the local market. This explains why, in regions that produce the finest coffees in the world, you can find customers in restaurants being served well-known brands of instant coffee,

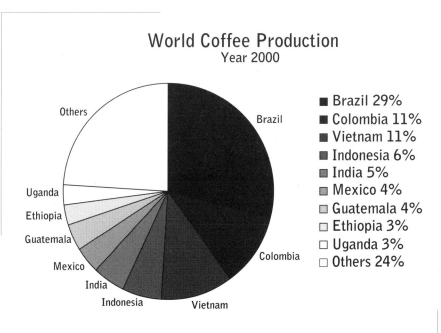

World Coffee Production
Year 2000

- Brazil 29%
- Colombia 11%
- Vietnam 11%
- Indonesia 6%
- India 5%
- Mexico 4%
- Guatemala 4%
- Ethiopia 3%
- Uganda 3%
- Others 24%

Source: International Coffee Organization (ICO): www.ico.org, October, 2001.

which is made with inferior grades of coffee.

In recent years, export markets in many coffee-producing countries have been privatized. Initially, this led to a large increase in the number of exporters, but in Mexico, after several years of privatization only the most "efficient" exporters have remained in business, creating a virtual monopoly.[19]

Although the various coyotes have considerable influence on markets in coffee-producing countries, their importance on the international stage is limited. Globally, prices are determined by the New York and London commodity exchanges.

LINK 5: THE BROKER

Practically the entire world trade in coffee, grown in the South, is controlled in two Northern centres: the New York exchange, which deals in *Arabica* coffee, and the London exchange, which handles the trade in *Robusta*.

Brokers are international businesspeople who buy and sell on commission without ever owning or handling the coffee that they trade. Brokers act as intermediaries between exporters and importers. Giant multinational corporations such as Nestlé or Philip Morris (owner of Kraft General Foods) have their own brokers. The huge buying and selling power of these corporations allows them to speculate and exercise great influence on the coffee exchanges.

Brokers have access to an ultramodern information network. If, for example, a satellite study predicts extreme weather conditions in Brazil (the world's largest coffee producer), the price of coffee on world markets will rise.[20] However, if an excellent harvest is forecast, world prices will fall. Rumours and psychological factors play a large role in determining market prices.

As the following graph shows, the price of coffee fluctuates considerably from one year to the next, affecting the income of coffee producers. Meanwhile, the price paid by consumers for their morning brew rarely falls as much.

Price Fluctuations
Green Bean vs Retail Prices

Source: Thomson, Bob. 2001. Using Statistics Canada's data on roasted and ground coffee (Time Series P2164). Also: Food and Agriculture Organization (FAO) www.fao.org. Also: New York Board Of Trade (NYBOT): www.nybot.com

LINK 6: THE ROASTER

The companies whose brand names appear on the coffee we buy usually roast and distribute the product. Over the past decade, these companies have become increasingly concentrated in the hands of giant agro-food corporations. Although you may find 15 or 20 brands of coffee on the supermarket shelf, the majority are owned by a few large multinationals. In 2001, 45 percent of the world coffee market was controlled by just three corporations: Philip Morris, Nestlé and Sara Lee.[21] As globalization continues, this concentration of the market increases.

By purchasing hundreds of thousands of tonnes of coffee at a time, large corporations are able to benefit from an enormous economy of scale and reduce their retail costs. The influence they hold over the world market and the economies of coffee-producing countries is undeniable. As mentioned in Chapter 1, the annual sales of some of these corporations is greater than the gross domestic product of many of the countries that produce the original coffee beans. Predictably, the headquarters of these corporations are found in Northern countries, where the greater part of the profits remain.

Although the global coffee market is dominated by a handful of multinational corporations, recent years have witnessed the emergence of small independent roasters dedicated to quality coffee. It is these speciality coffee roasters who have shown the greatest openness to "sustainable" coffees (fair-trade, organic and shade-grown). In the United States, the Specialty Coffee Association of America (SCAA) has played a leading role in developing these niche markets. The notion of quality coffee is starting to be redefined to include environmental and social sustainability, thanks to the commitment of coffee roasters such as Café Campesino, Green Mountain Coffee and Thanksgiving Coffee, to mention but a few.

COFFEE ROASTING

The familiar aroma of coffee does not appear until the beans have been roasted at high temperatures. This causes the beans to go through a chemical transformation which gives them a brown, semi-black or black colour, depending upon the duration of the process. During the process, the beans are kept in constant motion in order to prevent burning or uneven roasting. Once adequately roasted, the beans are quickly cooled.

The final quality of the coffee is affected greatly by this stage of processing. For this reason, coffee-roasting companies invest in the most modern equipment that can precisely control the temperature, humidity and roasting time of each bean.

Once roasted, coffee loses its freshness rapidly. Ideally, in order to preserve the coffee's flavour, beans are not roasted until just prior to sale.

LINK 7: THE RETAILER

Most consumers make the final choice of what coffee goes in their cup in front of the supermarket shelves or the coffee-shop counter. This apparently innocuous moment is the target of vast sums spent on advertising and design.

Supermarkets often use coffee as a "loss leader." Sold at a special price, it brings in customers who buy other items while they are there. Like all other sectors of the agro-food industry, the retail market is becoming concentrated in the hands of a shrinking number of players. There are fewer and fewer small independent grocery stores, while the big ones are becoming gigantic and increasingly inter-linked.

As for places to sit and enjoy a cup of coffee, the past few years have seen a proliferation of coffee shops, contributing to the growth of the gourmet-coffee market. As with wine, there are connoisseurs, but many ordinary people derive a simple pleasure from savouring the bitter drink served in every fashion, from cappuccino to espresso, from latté to allongé. As much as the beverage, these coffee shops are selling an *ambiance*, a "lifestyle choice," which is a small luxury within most people's reach.

THE WEALTH OF NATIONS?
OR CORPORATIONS?

Multinationals dominate the coffee trade, with sales figures that exceed the gross domestic product of many coffee-producing nations. As their overriding motivation is to make short-term profits for their shareholders, multinationals invest little in the development or environmental sustainability of these countries.

Comparison between GDPs of coffee-producing countries and the annual sales of multinational corporations

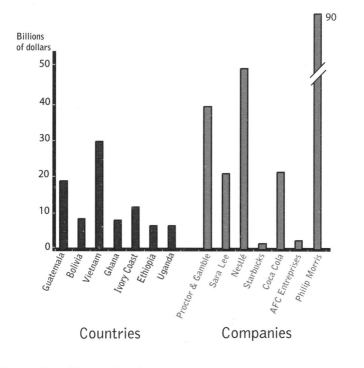

Source: United Nations Development Programme (UNDP). *Human Development Report 2001*. New York: UNDP, 2001. Also: Annual reports of companies for the year 2000.

Although it has become common to pay more than $2 for a cup of good coffee, this is not to the benefit of coffee-producing regions. In 1985, 38 percent of the retail price of coffee sold in the US went to the producing countries, where it was shared between intermediaries and producers. In 1995, the figure had fallen to 23 percent,[22] a 40 percent drop over ten years. Over the same period the retail price of coffee rose by 30 percent.

With the growth of gourmet coffee sales, retailers' margins have increased, giving them an opportunity to include fair-trade products in their menu.

LINK 8: WE, THE CONSUMERS

Coffee has been popular in North America for at least two centuries. Roughly a fifth of all the coffee grown worldwide ends up in the USA, the largest coffee-consuming country.[23]

An anecdotal tradition ascribes Americans' preference for coffee over tea to the famous "Boston Tea Party" of 1773 when, as frustration with British taxation and import policies reached its peak shortly before the American Revolution, a cargo of tea was thrown into Boston harbour. As a result, the tradition goes, choosing coffee over tea was a patriotic gesture. It would seem that coffee drinking involved a political choice at that time. As we will see, history is repeating itself today, as people begin to choose fair-trade, organic or shade-grown coffee for political reasons, but this time on a global scale.

Today, coffee is found in every corner store or restaurant. Drunk by people of every age, lifestyle and background, it is available in many flavours and at widely differing prices—especially since the recent boom of fashionable coffee-shop chains.

The fact that it is drunk by almost everybody makes coffee one of the world's most valuable commodities and, as we have seen, gives the big players in the coffee trade an enormous influence over the world market, and hence over the lives of producers in Southern countries. But the same popularity of coffee gives us, the consumers, enormous power to change things by exercising our freedom to choose what coffee we purchase. By insisting on fair-trade coffee, we can make a real difference to the lives of many people. This will be shown in the next chapter, which presents the concrete example of small coffee-growing families uniting in the *Unión de Comunidades Indígenas de la Región del Istmo*, or UCIRI (Union of Indigenous Communities of the Isthmus Region).

THE EFFECTS OF COFFEE ON HEALTH

Although it may be habit-forming, coffee is not an essential food item. In fact, some health practitioners suggest restricting coffee consumption in order to improve personal health.[24] Like tea, certain carbonated drinks and certain medications, coffee contains caffeine, a nervous-system stimulant that can prevent sleep. Excessive consumption may also cause anxiety and affect bodily coordination.[25] Evidently, the effects of coffee vary from one person to the next, and some are much more sensitive than others. Consumed in moderation though, coffee is rarely associated with extreme side-effects,[26] and it generally recognized that it can have a positive stimulating effect.

WHO OWNS THE BRANDS WE BUY?

• Philip Morris (USA)

Coffee business
A.D.C.
Blendy
BRIM
Cafe 1686
Cafe Sperl
Carte Noire
Electra-Perk
General Foods
International Coffees
Gevalia
GrandMère
Kaffee HAG
Jacobs Krönung
Jacobs Monarch
Jacques Vabre
Kenco
Maxim
Maxwell House
Mellow Roast
Nabob
Private Collection
Saimaza
Sanka
Splendid
Super Roast
The Spirit of Coffee
Traditional Roast
Yuban
Distributes all
Starbucks coffee in
supermarkets.

Some other food products
Claussen
Di Giorno
Jell-O
Kool-aid
All the Kraft food
products.
Minute Rice
Nabisco
Oscar Mayer
Philadelphia
Post cereals
Tang
Toblerone, etc.

Cigarettes
Basic
Benson & Hedges
Marlboro
Merit
Parliament
Virginia Slims, etc.

Beers
Icehouse
Miller
Milwaukee's Best
Molson USA (majority ownership)
Molson Canada (important interest)
Red Dog, etc.

• Procter & Gamble (USA)

Coffee business
Brothers
Epic
Flavor Filter
Folger's
High Point
Mountain Grown
Millstone

Some other food products
Crisco
Olean
Pringles, etc.

Other products
Always
Ariel
Cover Girl
Crest
Didronel
Head & Shoulders
Oil of Olay
Pampers
Pantene Pro-V
Tampax
Tide
Vicks
Whisper, etc.

• Cara (Canada)
Coffee business
Main shareholder of
Second Cup (but coffee roasted by Kraft
General Foods.

Food services
Beaver Foods
Limited
Café & Grill
Cara Airport
Services
Cara Health Services
Harvey's
Summit Food
Service Distributors
Swiss Chalet
Toast!

•Nestlé (Switzerland)

Coffee business
Bonka
Brava
Cains
Chase & Sanborn
Clasico
Dolca
Ristreto Classic
Columbian Select
European Roast
Flavor Roast
Gold Blend
Goodhost
High Yield
Hills Brothers
Loumidis
Maragor Bold
MJB
Mountain Blend
Nescafé
Panache
Perfect Balance
Ricoffy
Ricoré
Sark's
Silka
Sunrise
Taster's Choice
Zoégas

Some other food products
Carnation
Findus
Friskies
Libby's
Maggi
Nestea
Nestlé ice cream & chocolate bars:

Aero,
After Eight,
Drumstick,
Kit-Kat,
Smarties, etc.
Perrier
Stouffer's
Vittel, etc.

Other products:
Alcon
L'Oréal (important interest).

•Starbucks (USA)

Coffee business
Starbucks
Caffee Gemma
Coffee Connection
Espresso Luna
Frappuccino
Kontakt
Proteo
Tazo Tea.

•Diedrich (USA)

Coffee business
Coffee Plantation
Diedrich
Coffee People
Gloria Jean's
and franchise
agreements with
Cumberland Coffee
Co. and California
Coffee Co.

•AFC Enterprises (USA)

Coffee business
Chesapeake
Seattle's Best Coffee
Torrefazione
Chesapeake
Cinnabon

Food services
Popeye's
Church's Fried
Chicken

•Van Houtte (Canada)

Coffee business
Van Houtte
Christophe Van Houtte
Gérard Van Houtte
Orient Express
Café Pure
Red Carpet
Food Services
Café Séléna
Plantation
Les amoureux du café
Caracas Coffee Services
Filter Fresh
McQuarrie's Coffee Services (majority ownership)
The Coffee Group
Gold Cup Coffee Company Ltd
VKI Technologies

•Sara Lee (USA)

Coffee business and restaurants

Arabica & Robusta
Bravo
Café do Ponto
Café au lait, Caferto
Cafitesse
Cafuego
Chat Noir
Chock full o'Nuts
(which in turn owns
La Touraine
Quickava
River Road
Ireland Coffee and tea)
Continental
Décafé
Douwe Egberts
Emerald Cream
Finley
Friele
Gamelli
Gourmet Ground
Harris
Java Coast
Jacqmotte
Kanis & Gunnink
Laurentis
Maison du Café
Marcilla
Merrild, Metropolitan
Mildcafé
Moccona
Piazza
Piazza d'Oro
Pickwick
Prebica Estate Coffees
Pronto Café
Soley
Soleto
Seleto
Superior Coffee
Van Nelle Supra
Wechsler Coffee
World's Finest

Some other food products

Ball Park
Bryan
Hillshire Farm
Hygrade
Jimmy Dean
Justin Bridou
Paradise Tropical Teas
Pickwick tea
Sara Lee food products, etc.

Other products

Abanderado
Bali
Champion
Coach
Dim
DKNY
Donna Karan, Hanes
Hanes Her Way
Just My Size
Kiwi
L'eggs
Playtex
Princesa
Rinbros
Sara Lee products
Wonderbra, etc.

•Tetley (USA)

Coffee Business:

Bustelo
Martinson's
Oquendo
Also owns the
Schonbrunn Co.
(which in turn owns:
Brown Gold
Medaglia d'Oro
Savarin
Tenco)

Sources : Company annual reports for the year 2000. Also: Companies and their Brands. Vol. 1 A-K, Eighteenth Edition, Jennifer L. Carman & Christine A. Kesler, Gale Research, USA, 1998. Also: "Investir." Les Affaires, (February 22, 1997), No. 77. Also: Canadian Corporate News, May 4, 1999 Also: Investor's Report, Financial Post DataGroup, Toronto, January 2, 1999. Also: U.S. Security and Exchanges Commission Web page: www.sec.gov. Also: Procter & Gamble company form 10-K. September 9, 1998.

Notes

1. UNDP. op. cit. 1999.
2. Colombian Coffee Federation (FNC):
   www.juanvaldez.commenu/history/ethics.html
3. UNCTAD. *Coffee: An Exporter's Guide*. Geneva, 1992.
4. Rice and McLean. op. cit. 22.
5. Rice and McLean. op. cit. 11.
6. Greenfield, Myrna. "Alternative Trade: Giving Coffee a New Flavor:"
   Making Coffee Strong. Equal Exchange: Boston, 1993, 7-12.
7. Dewey, K. G. *Nutrition Consequences of the Transfer from Subsistence to
   Commercial Agriculture in Tabasco: Food Energy in Tropical Ecosystems*,
   New York: Gordon and Breach Science Publisher. 105-144, 1985. Also:
   Institute for Agriculture and Trade Policy (IATP): www.iatp.org
8. Rice and McLean. op. cit. 11.
9. Personal visits to coffee plantations in Mexico, October-November 2000.
10. Museo Nacional de Culturas Populares. op. cit.
11. INEGI. Anuario Estadístico del Estado de Oaxaca, Mexico, 1995. Also:
    UNDP. Human Development Report 1994, New York, 1994, 223.
12. Interview with Dr. Aurora Juez, Lachiviza, May 24, 1996.
13. Interview with Dr. Gregorio de Anda, San José el paraiso, May 30, 1996.
14. The Economist Intelligence Unit Limited. *EIU Country Report*, 2nd
    Quarter 1999, 5.
15. Dicum and Luttinger. op. cit. 54.
16. Brière, Julie et Ruby, Françoise. "Le top 10 des résidus de pesticides."
    Protégez-vous, (August 1995), 18.
17. Interview with Joel López Sánchez, engineer with Agroquimicos y
    Semillas del Sur, Oaxaca, Mexico, June 22, 1996.
18. Interview with Hanneke Kruit, San José el Paraiso. June 3, 1996.
19. Marlin, Christian. *Les stratégies des grands torréfacteurs et importateurs
    sur le marché international du café*. Paris: Max Havelaar France. May
    1993. 34.
20. Renard, María Cristina. *La Comercialización international del café*. Mexico
    City: Universidad Autonoma Chapingo. 1993, 48.
21. *Dow Jones International News*. "Coffee Cos. Gain from Globalization but
    See Shortfalls." May 21, 2001.
22. Dicum and Luttinger. op. cit. 112.
23. Ibid. 38.
24. Tortora, Gerard. *Principes d'anatomie et de physiologie*. Montréal: Centre
    Éducatif et Culturel. 1988.
25. Ramson, David. "What's Brewing." *New Internationalist* (September 1995)
    19. Also: Davids, Kenneth. *A Guide to Buying, Brewing and Enjoying*, San
    Francisco: 101 Productions, 1979.
26. Davids. op. cit.

Chapter 5
A Different Path for Coffee Growers

Rather than upholding a trade system that perpetuates the inequalities between North and South, fair trade offers a means to adjust the balance. It gives small producers a better price for their coffee while supporting sustainable development in the areas of environmental conservation, health care and education. Fair trade brings consumers closer to producers by eliminating numerous intermediaries. This system is built on justice, not charity.

As the diagram overleaf shows, fair-trade coffee is sold directly by producer cooperatives to an importer or a fair-trade organization (FTO). Cooperatives and buyers sign contracts in advance in order to ensure a decent price and a guaranteed market for producers, no matter what speculation or changes may occur on world markets. Certain FTOs pay for a portion of the harvest in advance or offer low-interest loans to the peasant organizations on request. As you will read in the next chapter, the history of fair trade is rich and goes far beyond just coffee. But let's start with the morning Java.

More than 330 coffee cooperatives in 18 countries take part in the fair-trade movement. Among then is the *Unión de Comunidades Indígenas de la Región del Istmo* (UCIRI) in

Mexico. Their story, like others, shows how fair trade helps peasants to break out of the cycle of dependence and exploitation that is common in the conventional coffee trade.

The Fair-Trade Route
From coffee tree to cup

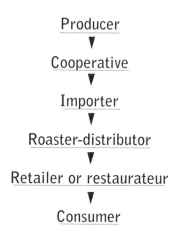

Producer
▼
Cooperative
▼
Importer
▼
Roaster-distributor
▼
Retailer or restaurateur
▼
Consumer

PRINCIPLES OF FAIR TRADE

1. Direct trade

Fair-trade organizations (FTOs) buy directly from cooperatives (or other FTOs). Producers and FTOs are equal commercial partners and treat each other with mutual respect and support. They share information freely and help each other in the pursuit of their respective goals.

2. Fair price

Producers and FTOs together fix a price that takes into account both the needs of Southern producers and the realities of Northern markets. Cooperatives must be paid a minimum of $2.77 per kg ($1.26 per lb.) for *Arabica* coffee and $2.42 per kg ($1.10 per lb.) for *Robusta*. If the market price is higher than these guaranteed prices, a premium of $0.023 per kg ($0.05 per lb.) is added to the market price. Producers must plan to recoup their production costs and make sufficient profit to cover their daily needs. The FTOs must be able to sell their product at a reasonable price. FTOs pay a higher price for organic coffee.

3. Long-term commitment

Cooperatives can count on FTOs to buy their product on a regular basis, allowing them to better plan their operations.

4. Credit

Credit at low rates of interest can be granted to a cooperative that requests it, for up to 60 percent of the value of the contract. This may take the form of prepayment for a proportion of orders. In practice, however, relatively few producers receive credit from their buyers.

5. Democratic management

Producers must divide profits equitably. All workers in the producer cooperatives must have a voice in the decision-making process and the way in which the group is organized.

6. Public information

FTOs supply consumers with information on producers and the need to support fair trade. The financial records of FTOs should be open to the public.

7. Environmental conservation and community development

FTOs support producers who practise sustainable agriculture and who have a community-development plan. Most cooperatives in the fair-trade network use no chemical pesticides or fertilizers, which entails more work for producers; however, they are not necessarily certified organic, since certification involves extra costs for the producers. Most coffee is grown under the shade of the forest, preserving the habitats of fauna and flora.

See Appendix A for details of the criteria for the certification of fair-trade coffee established by Fairtrade Labelling Organizations International (FLO-International).

UNIÓN DE COMUNIDADES INDIGENAS DE LA REGIÓN DEL ISTMO (UCIRI)

In the Mexican State of Oaxaca, a group of peasants have chosen to take a stand and to act for the future of their communities. To protect the Earth, which they call their mother, these indigenous Zapotecos, Mixes, and Chontales practice organic agriculture under the shade of the forest.

Source: Waridel, Laure. *Coffee with a Cause: Moving Towards Fair Trade*. Montréal: Les Intouchables, 1997, 38.

UCIRI: AN EXAMPLE OF A COOPERATIVE

The indigenous peoples of the Istmo region of Oaxaca in Southern Mexico began to cultivate coffee about 100 years ago, but continued to grow corn, black beans, peppers, other vegetables, and some fruit to meet their own food needs.

From the beginning, selling their coffee proved difficult. Without any means of transport, they relied on merchants who used mules or horses to be able to get to the coffee producers' small mountainous villages, buy the coffee at low prices, and carry it back to the larger centre of Ixtepec. By the end of the 1970s, roads had opened up several villages to buyers from the Mexican Coffee Institute (INMECAFE), a government marketing organization. This improved the situation somewhat, but only temporarily. The peasants were encouraged to take out high-interest loans in order to purchase newly developed seed varieties, fertilizers and pesticides. Although some growers managed to increase their harvests, low coffee prices, coupled with debts, meant that the situation of most families improved little. The temporary improvements offered by the various chemicals gave way to long-term health and environmental problems.

THE INDIGENOUS PEOPLES

Oaxaca is Mexico's most ethnically diverse State, with half its population belonging to 16 different indigenous groups.[1] UCIRI members are Zapotecos, Mixteco and Chontales. Each group's language, traditional dress and customs have evolved over the past 10,000 years.[2]

As early as 500 BC, the Zapotecos founded Monte-Alban, probably the first city in the Americas. At that time they practised agriculture, and had domesticated corn and black beans. They also followed three types of calendars based on the agricultural cycle, religious celebrations, and astrological movements.

Indigenous cultures are still very much alive today and many traditional practices form the basis for social, economic and political activity in the communities. *Tequio* is a system of voluntary community service performed by all members for collective projects involving, for example, access to drinking water, construction of schools and other activities.[3] *Usos y costumbres* (uses and customs) is the name given to the present political system in the majority of indigenous communities. Municipal delegates and other village representatives are elected by assemblies composed of one member of each family, traditionally the husband or father. This system does not involve political parties; instead, it emphasizes equal responsibility for each member and the welfare of the collective.[4]

Changes in the community, as a result of both internal and external influences, are omnipresent. These changes often occur very rapidly. Among the factors challenging the existing traditional social, economic and political systems are: access to roads; the availability of new products; the introduction of the party political system; the arrival of new religious groups, alcohol, illegal drugs, and the concept of agriculture for export; population growth; and ecological deterioration.

On the other hand, by the end of the 1960s several local organizations had begun to take shape. These organizations have been instrumental in reasserting the value of traditional knowledge, experience and skills. They have helped facilitate local people's efforts to take control of their development. A number of these groups have formed associations nationally and internationally. By working collectively, indigenous peoples have raised their profile, bringing positive changes to the community, including an improved standard of living.

Éric St-Pierre

The first steps

In 1981, a team of liberation-theology Catholic missionaries organized a meeting with the Istmo coffee growers to analyze the peasants' plight. The community came to the following conclusions, set out below in their own words:

- *The price of coffee is too low and does not allow us to respond to basic needs.*
- *Banks do not lend us money because we cannot pay the interest.*
- *We do not have enough to eat.*
- *We become sick easily and there is not enough medical care. The medicine offered to us is too expensive. We lose valuable working time and our families suffer due to these illnesses.*
- *Transportation is of poor quality and very expensive.*
- *Many villages have no access to potable water, electricity, telephone or even telegraph systems.*
- *The education our children receive is inadequate. The teachers are often absent.*
- *Our houses are in poor condition. We would like to renovate them or build new ones, but we don't have the money.*
- *Foodstore prices are too high and their shelves are often empty.*[5]

With the support of the missionaries from the parish of Guienagati and the diocese of Tehuantepec, a group of these peasants began actively seeking new outlets for their coffee. Their efforts were fairly successful, especially after 1983 when UCIRI gained status as a legally recognized entity and was allowed the right to export directly to the North. This helped to break the stranglehold of the many intermediaries. At this time, UCIRI was made up of families from 17 different communities.

In order to export directly, cooperative members had to learn the coffee trade:

"We had to learn how to calculate the weight of the coffee, to make receipts, and to procure sacks and trucks for transport. Some of us overcame our uneasiness about going into town, others learned to use the telephone for the first time... Before then, the only machines we used were small hand-mills and most people had never been to a large town."[6]

Export permits proved very difficult to obtain. Delegates returned empty-handed from trips to Oaxaca or even Mexico City, having also lost valuable working time. Furthermore, the cooperative was viewed with suspicion by coyotes as a peasant organization edging into their territory. UCIRI was labelled as subversive and communist by its opponents.[7] Members were subjected to intimidation and reprisals from local merchants and even the local and national civil servants and government.

UCIRI members have been subject to many vicious attacks: between 1985 and 1992, 39 men, women and children were murdered.[8] Their only crime was their effort to fight the poverty and exploitation they face by building a social organization. In March 1994, soldiers invaded the UCIRI agricultural school at San José el Paraiso. The government and local politicians falsely accused the organization of being a paramilitary training centre supporting the *Ejército Zapatista de Liberación National* (EZLN) in the adjoining State of Chiapas.

As Roberto Raygoza Beltran, an advisor to UCIRI, points out: "UCIRI's situation is not easy. It's difficult to keep people feeling motivated, especially when they feel threatened. It takes a great deal of courage to continue the struggle day after day."[9]

UCIRI developed its own transport system, breaking the local monopoly. Different products became more accessible and coffee could be shipped out of the villages more easily. But there was more: their presence on the roads gave them an inside view of the marijuana trade. UCIRI denounced this contraband, but this only served to make them more enemies among the ranks of coyotes and local-government officials, many of whom were involved in this trade themselves. It is an unfortunate fact that the drug trade played an important role in the region's economy and was the cause of much violence in the community.

International support
UCIRI has been successful in generating support outside Mexico. Thanks to the help of Father Franz Van der Hoff, a Dutch priest actively involved with UCIRI, contacts were established with fair-trade organizations, at first in Holland (S.O.S.) and Germany (GEPA), and later in other European countries and in North America. These organizations do more than just purchase the coffee directly from UCIRI at a higher price. They also support peasants in their efforts to improve the quality of their coffee and to find their way in the international coffee trade.[10]

A participatory democracy
UCIRI is a union of community members. Every community has its own representative, elected by direct vote at UCIRI community meetings. The delegate is responsible for attending meetings at the end of each month at organization headquarters. Upon returning to the community, the delegate explains the proceedings of the meeting to the local board of directors and the family producers active in UCIRI. Representatives of the families (generally the head of the family, either a man or woman) attend the meetings.

Within UCIRI communities, there are also boards in charge of organizing monthly community meetings, reviewing the general assembly's compliance with agreements, dealing with organization finances and other activities. Duties are delegated to security and implementation committees for various projects such as transportation, savings and credit funds, health, organic agriculture, mills, organized communal work, internal inspections and others. UCIRI also orchestrates new projects that have a significant impact on the communities, such as garment making and organic marmalades.

UCIRI has a central board of directors that is responsible for implementing decisions made at the meetings. It has three members: a president, a secretary and a treasurer. There is also a security board. Every three years, in full view of all assembly members, active UCIRI members in a direct vote elect the members of the central administrative board and the security board. UCIRI members occupying important positions do not receive any extra revenue. Positions are seen as a way in which producers can provide beneficial services to the organization.

Membership in UCIRI entails an investment of time. Participation in meetings and other local projects is obligatory. In villages where a large number of families are UCIRI members, jobs are divided among a greater number of people, thus lightening everyone's overall workload. In villages where few families are involved, however, the time commitment for members is greater.

Cliserio Villanueva Solana, UCIRI president in the community of Guadalupe, explains: "We have few difficulties here, because the members themselves decide on our course of action... each has his say, and regardless of our individual opinions, together we decide what is best for all of us. Here there is democracy, equality and respect for ourselves and each other."

Many communities in UCIRI are Zapoteco, a matriarchal indigenous group in which women traditionally controlled most of the family's social and economic affairs. This changed after the arrival of the Europeans, who imposed their patriarchal system. Men from the cities convinced the Zapoteco peasants to grow coffee, causing a further shift in the balance of power within the family. As a result, although UCIRI sets out to be democratic and inclusive, in most cases families are represented at meetings of the cooperative by men. People are aware of the imbalance and are trying to encourage women to become more involved in projects at the decision-making level, rather than merely in the work of carrying out projects. Women's groups have been formed, fostering greater participation by the entire community. As Franz Van der Hoff explains,

UCIRI's RULES OF OPERATION

"Our organization is open to all peasants who want to fight to improve their quality of life and are prepared to abide by UCIRI's principles and rules."

1. Agree to be an active member.
2. Attend monthly meetings and training courses given occasionally in the community of Lachiviza and the CEC *(Centro de educacion campesina)*
3. Refrain from consuming alcohol during official meetings at Lachiviza or Ixtepec.
4. Be completely honest.
5. Do not behave like a coyote, even a small coyote [do not buy or resell the coffee of other producers].
6. Sell only your own coffee: do not even sell your brother's, uncle's, or friend's coffee.
7. Do not become involved in any potentially compromising organizations.
8. Be a genuine peasant.
9. Do not act opportunistically for personal gain.
10. If you misbehave, you will face expulsion from the Union. The meeting will decide whether members can re-join the Union, on a case-by-case basis.
11. Do not grow marijuana or any other crops related to the drug trade.
12. Do not own military equipment.
13. Use no chemical fertilizers or pesticides.
14. Make and use organic fertilizers (compost).
15. Undertake to fulfil your cultural obligations.
16. Be prepared to give a helping hand when required.
17. Be prepared to support UCIRI's objectives, which lie not only in fighting for coffee but also for life, health, home, organized communal work projects, organic agriculture, local schools, etc.

Source: Free translation from UCIRI.-*¿Quiénes Somos?, Nuestro Caminar*, Pasos No. 28, November 1991, 41-42.

women's participation in the democratic process can also be seen from another perspective:

> *"In the valley more than in the sierra, the Zapotecos have strong matriarchal customs. Even though men attend the meetings, this does not necessarily mean that they have the last word. We discovered that the meetings lasted for two days because the Marianos and Gueveanos would consult their wives and sometimes return the second day with a decision that was the opposite of what had been suggested on the first. Although this tradition is not as strong as it once was, women continue to play an extremely important role and are active participants in the assembly with their own board of directors."*

UCIRI's PROJECTS

Higher income from coffee production will not alone solve day-to-day problems in the communities. As a result, the income UCIRI receives from selling coffee is not only distributed among the coffee producers, but is also used to finance a variety of community projects designed to improve the quality of life for the people of the Istmo region.

Moving towards organic agriculture

The subtropical forest is a complex and fragile ecosystem. The population of the Istmo region is growing and consequently agricultural activities are intensifying.

An elder in the village of Guadalupe described how 30 years ago, farmers practised crop rotation over a 15- to 20-year cycle. To begin each cycle, the land was cleared by burning the trees and brush, the ashes serving as fertilizer. Over the following years, successive varieties of vegetables were grown, after which the soil was left fallow for several years before vegetable crops were grown again. As the population in the region has risen, the time that the soil can be left to regenerate has been reduced. Today, the same parcels of land are burned every three to seven years, which does not allow the soil to regenerate. The condition of the soil has

UCIRI's ORGANIZATIONAL STRUCTURE

Economy
management
coffee production and trade
improved stoves
low-interest loans
food store
hardware store
common transportation system
organic jam
clothing manufacture
small coffee roaster

Education
agricultural school
training sessions

Health
natural medicine
nutrition
prevention
hygiene

Environment
organic agriculture
horticulture
fish farming
compost
recycling

Development projects

Central board of directors

Local board of directors in each of the 52 communities

2,349 families

deteriorated progressively, contributing to major erosion problems that have had damaging effects on the habitat of regional flora and fauna, an important part of the overall ecosystem.

Chemical fertilizers and pesticides were introduced in order to increase soil productivity and combat plant and insect pests. The Mexican government has set up "peasant-support" programs designed to encourage the use of these chemical products. Many peasants feel that the real beneficiaries of these programs are the agrochemical companies.

Because of the dangers of pesticide use, the peasants involved in UCIRI have opted for organic agriculture. Each community has an organic advisor whose task is to teach organic techniques and also discourage the traditional burning methods. This person is responsible for a demonstration plot where everyone works collectively to develop new techniques, not only for coffee but also for corn, black beans and other crops.

In comparison with conventional chemical agriculture, organic farming entails more work, knowledge, and care of the soil. Farmers have to clear the land by hand, make compost and plant a wide variety of plants that either enrich the soil or act as natural protection against various insects or diseases. Shade trees are left or planted around the coffee trees; they not only offer protection from the sun, but also help to maintain soil humidity. Terraces made of wood, stone or plants are also built up to reduce erosion.

Although organic agriculture demands more work of the peasants, it also offers greater rewards. The quality of their coffee is superior, the price they receive for their products is higher and the equilibrium of their soils is maintained. Organic methods allow local fauna and flora to flourish, thereby protecting biodiversity. They also provide a diversity of resources for the family such as a wide variety of fruits and grains as well as wood. Human needs can thus be fulfilled while an ecological balance is maintained. Organic farming is a very concrete way to avoid the uncounted environmental and social costs usually entailed in the conventional coffee-production system.

An agricultural school in the forest

In 1986, UCIRI set up an independent agricultural school without support from the Mexican government. The *Centro de educación campesina* (CEC) is the only agricultural school in the mountains. Twenty-five young men and women are enrolled in the school each year; after their one-year training they return to their communities to share their new knowledge.

The school's program is based on the realities of peasant life. They learn how to better understand their mountainous environment and its vegetation, soil types and animal life. In addition, they study sustainable methods of agriculture that they can apply not only to coffee production, but also to other crops and livestock production in order to improve the family diet. It is often these students who play the role of organic advisors upon their return to their communities.

A clinic in the mountains

As mentioned earlier, health problems are a major preoccupation for many of the rural families in the Istmo region. UCIRI has established a health unit, consisting of a doctor and over 40 volunteer "health promoters," to work on illness prevention. The unit offers workshops that teach participants to use local and natural resources. For example, they learn how to improve and balance their diet, how to achieve better general hygiene and how to recognize and use local medicinal herbs.

The health promoters are women and men from UCIRI's communities who show a particular interest in health care. They receive continuous training from the fully qualified physician. They volunteer their time to promote health care for all members of their community, members of UCIRI and non-members alike.

Thanks to the support of other institutions such as the *Universidad Metropolitana*, UCIRI has been able to facilitate access to specific health services such as dental examinations.

Collective work

Trabajo Común Organizado (organized communal work) was started with the aim of dealing concretely with regional economic problems. This project has put an end to the coyotes' monopolies on transportation and high-interest loans, and the exorbitant prices charged in local stores.

Initial funding for these projects came from Canadian and Dutch sources. With added support provided by fair-trade organizations, this money has allowed UCIRI to make low-interest loans available to communities for a variety of development projects. One such project involved purchasing several trucks and buses to provide a transport system linking the major regional centres. This is how the UPZMI cooperative transport system started.

In addition, cooperative stores have been started in several communities. Collective buying has allowed these stores to achieve tremendous economies of scale which, in turn, allow products to be sold for lower prices and break the monopolies previously held by the local elite. Most importantly, the cooperative stores have given peasants in the region better access to food.

A collective corn mill, necessary for the preparation of tortilla dough, has been built in every community. This eases the daily work of women. However, horticultural projects aimed at improving nutrition have yet to offer major results, apparently because of a shortage of technical knowledge, seeds, time and other resources.

UCIRI provides workshops on a wide number of topics, including how to build a dry toilet or wood stove that burns less fuel, as well as how to prepare nutritious meals. Most of UCIRI's projects have been organized at the community level using simple techniques and readily available materials. The benefits of these projects are felt throughout the community, and not only among people who are members of UCIRI.

New projects
UCIRI conceives of development as a multi-dimensional under-taking, and this is the source of its inexhaustible creativity in finding small answers to producers' big questions. In recent years, the organization has implemented two new projects. One is a clothing factory in the city of Ixtepec (funded with low-interest loans from the National Fund for the Social Economy (FONAES) and the Dutch bank Rabobank) to provide jobs to the producers' children, who would otherwise migrate to the cities and abroad in search of better opportunities. This plant has generated more than 120 direct jobs.

The other project concerns the production of organic jam. Depending on coffee as the sole source of income is risky, and so the organization has been introducing new crops such as black-berry, raspberry and passionfruit for organic jams. It also pro-duces jam from the fruit of the region's native trees, including soursop, mamey and banana, which do double duty as coffee shade trees.

UCIRI is also progressively moving into production of roasted ground coffee, a product for which domestic demand is growing.

A broader base
During its 18 years of history, membership has risen from about 100 people at the outset to 2,349 members in 53 com-munities at present. UCIRI has grown because its members have taken it upon themselves to work together to improve their future prospects. UCIRI has already inspired the creation of similar organizations in the neighbouring Mexican state of Chiapas, in Costa Rica, Peru, Colombia and several other coun-tries.

PORTRAIT OF **UCIRI**

Founded: 1983
Number of families involved: 2,349
Ethnic groups: Zapoteco, Mixe, Mixteco, and Chontal
Cultivated lands: an average per family of 2 to 5 hectares (5 to 12 acres) for coffee trees and 5 to 8 hectares (25 to 30 acres) for subsistence crops
Type of organization: cooperative, one representative per family. General Assembly of delegates. Decision made by consensus
Coffees produced: *Arabica pergamino* and *A. capulin*
Agricultural method: organic, certified by the German organization Naturland and by Certimex in Mexico. Shade-grown.
Main buyers: GEPA (Germany), Equal Exchange (USA), CTM (Italy), A. Van Weely VB (Netherlands), EZA (Austria), Magasins du Monde (several European countries), Werchi (Switzerland), Just Us! (Canada)

WHAT ELSE IS GOING ON IN MEXICO?

The movement for fair-trade, organic and shade-grown coffee (and also other products) is particularly strong in Mexico, and UCIRI is far from being the only player. A number of organizations are involved in diverse projects, from capacity building and technical assistance on the ground to certification and marketing procedures.

Others are striving to develop the fair-trade system for the local market rather than merely for export. Several producer-consumer linkage initiatives in the form of speciality cafes have originated from the producers themselves. The cafes include La Selva, Biocafé, El Museo del Café and Café de Nuestra Tierra. In other cases, small Mexican producers have decided to work together to promote fair-trade, organic and shade-grown coffee domestically.

As made clear in the previous chapters, a great deal of work is needed to counter the social and environmental havoc created by the low price of coffee. However, a growing level of cooperation between the various initiatives discussed above is reinforcing the movement.

Comercio Justo Mexico

Mexico has a large number of small producers: some 250,000 small coffee producers, 50,000 beekeepers and more than 3 million basic-grain producers. In the current economic environment, these small producers are confronted with numerous obstacles to the marketing of their products: stiff international competition, price and market instability, lack of access to infrastructure and credit, and insufficient resources for promoting sustainable development, among others. Mexican small producers have fought for decades to overcome these obstacles; many of them have considerably augmented their productive and market capacity in the face of adverse conditions. Fair trade, both domestically and internationally, has played an important role in this progress. Fair-trade certification, particularly for coffee and honey, has helped to strengthen Mexican small producers' organizations as well as the home and community economies of their members.

In late 1998, a group of small producers and civic organizations decided to push ahead with the idea of creating a fair-trade certification system for the Mexican market. Based on various international experiences with fair trade, this group considered it important to promote fair trade on the domestic Mexican market which, with a population of nearly 100 million, constitutes an enormous market for small Mexican producers, even for those who have the opportunity to sell to the international fair-trade market. In May 1999, the organization *Comercio Justo Mexico* commenced operations and quickly set up a fair-trade certification body called *Sello Mexicano de Comercio Justo*.

Certimex

Certimex is a Mexican certification body for environmentally friendly products and processes. It was created in 1997 in response to producers' need for a local organic-certification entity. This new body should indeed meet the producers' expectations for access to organic certification at a lower cost and with domestic inspectors. For now, Certimex is focusing primarily on environmental certification; however, it expects to extend its activities to other areas, such as monitoring of fair-trade control systems and quality certification of farm products, to be developed jointly with *Comercio Justo Mexico*. The overall objective is to provide consumers with a guarantee that Certimex products are of high quality and adhere to fair-trade practices. Currently Certimex works with 85 organic-production projects involving approximately 17,000 producers, the majority of them aboriginal peasants in the states of Chiapas and Oaxaca.

MORE FAIR-TRADE AND ORGANIC-PRODUCTION ORGANIZATIONS

In Mexico, more than 30 organizations are practising fair trade and organic agriculture. Some of them are listed below.

ISMAM (Sierra Madre de Motozintla Aboriginal Producers' Association)

This association of aboriginal people from the region of Soconusco, Chiapas numbers about 1,300 members. With the support of UCIRI, it began production of organic coffee in 1986 and in 1990 published a practical handbook on growing organic coffee. ISMAM has promoted the development of direct links with the buyers, and its other projects include coffee storage and marketing, technical assistance, organized community work and healthcare projects. It supports a number of groups, such as *K'nan Choch Nuestra Madre Tierra*, which has a Certimex-certified project to produce organic potatoes and *chayote* for domestic consumption. ISMAM is also certified by Germany's *Naturland* and Switzerland's *IMO-Control*.

Union de Ejidos de la Selva (Union of Forest Settlements)

This organization began producing organic coffee in 1991 and now has approximately 1,200 members. Its initiatives include opening cafes for the sale of coffee directly from the producer. Café La Selva has opened outlets in Mexico City, San Cristobal de las Casas, Chiapas and Catalonia, Spain. It is certified by *Naturland* and *IMO-Control* as well as *Certimex*. The organization has other projects on storage and marketing, technical assistance, coffee drying (UNCAFESUR, with the participation of other Chiapas organizations), peasant women (gardens, bakeries, hominy mills, workshops, etc.), housing, etc.

Unión de Ejidos San Fernando (Union of Settlements of San Fernando)

This organization recently began organic production and has several projects relating to storage, marketing, technical assistance and cooperatives, a clothing factory and its own cafe, called Biocafé, located in the city of Tuxtla Gutierrez, Chiapas. Its members consist of over 1,000 small coffee producers. It is certified by *Naturland, IMO-Control* and *Certimex*, and is also a member of the alternative-trade organization *FLO International*.

CEPCO (Oaxaca Coffee Producers' Association)

This federation has approximately 23,000 members. It is one of the most tangibly successful examples of what organized small producers can do, now that it is listed in the FLO Registry (the registry of Fairtrade Labelling Organizations—see p. 154). CEPCO is composed of 43 grassroots organizations from all the coffee-producing areas of the State of Oaxaca. Its prime objective is to support marketing. For that purpose it has set up several legal entities, which have enabled it to cut operating costs for storage and marketing. It has other projects such as organic coffee production, organizing with women, "backyard medicine," clothing production, technical assistance and training. CEPCO sells its own coffee at Café Caracola, a store/cafe located in the city of Oaxaca. It is certified by *Naturland, IMO-Control, Certimex* and OCIA in the United States.

Majomut

Majomut, founded in 1982 and representing about 800 producer members, is located in the Altos de Chiapas region of Mexico. Its projects include coffee storage and marketing, technical assistance, organic coffee, corn-cultivation methods involving mulching, gardening, a small roasting project, a coffee museum and cafe in San Cristobal de las Casas, Chiapas, and a video project. It is a member of *FLO International* and is certified by *Naturland, IMO-Control,* and *Certimex.*

Tiemelonlá Nich K'lum Producers' Association

One of the largest grassroots organization in the Palenque, Chiapas region, grouping together approximately 580 producers. Its projects concern coffee storage and marketing, organized community work, organic coffee and corn, technical assistance, biological control of the coffee-bean borer (a coffee pest), mass production of seedlings, health care and others. At first, it received support from UCIRI to set up its organic program. It is a member of *FLO International* and is certified by *Naturland, IMO-Control,* and *Certimex.*

Kiee Lu'u Producers' Association

This organization is a clear example to show that there are many other possibilities besides coffee. This group of organic hibiscus producers is one of the few that has successfully marketed a product other than coffee on the alternative market. With approximately 87 producer members, all in the town of Zenzontepec, an area considered marginal in the State of Oaxaca, they have managed to make progress with a project formerly thought to be impossible. They market their product through a buyer on the German alternative market and are certified by *Naturland, IMO-Control,* and *Certimex.*

Mut Vitz

The cooperative Mut Vitz (which means "bird mountain" in Tzotzil) is comprised of some 1,000 indigenous Tzotzil farmers from 28 communities located in the Autonomous Region of San Juan de la Libertad in the highlands of Chiapas. It is a fine example of how local initiatives work collectively to achieve respect for indigenous rights and human dignity as well as seeking practical, economic solutions for their members.

Self-organized and administered by its elected representatives, Mut Vitz was registered in the FLO producer list in 1999 and is currently primed for organic certification by Certimex/Naturland. Mut Vitz exports its coffee to the United States, Canada and several European countries, as well as selling a significant amount of locally roasted and packaged coffee on the national market.

MAKING THE ALTERNATIVES KNOWN

Some organizations are attempting to establish links between consumers and producers in order to facilitate fairer trade practices. One of them, *Bio,* founded in 1991, focuses on environmental education and changing consumer habits. Through workshops, consulting activities, publications and pamphlets, including one on the "3 Rs" (Reduce, Reuse, Recycle), it reaches out to various groups, such as schools in Mexico City. It also publicizes and sells organic products such as coffee, honey, jam

and cleaning products at various points in the city. Through its workshops, *Bio* teaches how to make products such as bags, purses, T-shirts and belts from recycled materials. Along with other environmental and conservation organizations such as *Naturalia* and *Ecomorelia, Bio* has embarked on a major-awareness raising project in Mexico.

Similarly, *Cafe de Nuestra Tierra* is a project that seeks to increase the consumption of organic and conventional coffees grown by aboriginal producers, as well as to promote the drinking of herbal teas. It is made up of 12 regional member organizations of the National Association of Coffee Producing Organizations (CNOC) in the states of Chiapas, Oaxaca, Puebla, Guerrero, Veracruz and San Luis Potosí. Participating producers receive a fair price for their coffee without having to depend on intermediaries or speculative activity on the New York Stock Exchange. *Cafe de Nuestra Tierra* has a cafe in Mexico City where it sells coffee purchased directly from aboriginal producers.

If the fair-trade movement has been able to establish itself and to grow explosively in Mexico and abroad, it is thanks to the involvement of hundreds of thousands of people, not only in small mountain villages, but also in cities where people have been rallying to the cause and consuming fair-trade and organic coffee. Consuming has become a political act.

Before coffee could be exported directly, UCIRI needed a warehouse where beans could be shelled, graded and stored, as well as trucks to transport the goods to port. UCIRI established its own transport system which broke the local monopoly. This facilitated access to various goods and meant that coffee could leave the village more easily.

Notes

1. Diaz, Ximena Avellaneda. "Los grupos etnicos del estado de Oaxaca." *América Indigena*. Vol. 50. No 2, 1990. 8-9.

2. Winter, Marcus. "Periodo Prehispanico." In *Historia de la cuestion Agraria Mexicana: Estado de Oaxaca/Prehispanico-1924*. Mexico: Universidad autonoma Benito Juarez de Oaxaca. 1988. 23-106.

3. Winter. op. cit. 1990.

4. Diaz. op. cit. 1990.

5. UCIRI. "¿Quienes somos?", *Nuestro Caminar*, Ixtepec: UCIRI. Pasos No. 28, November 1991, 6.

6. Ibid, 9.

7. UCIRI. "Nuestra Historia", *Nuestra Caminar*, Ixtepec: UCIRI. Pasos No. 27, 1991.

8. Interview with Isaias Martinez Morales, former president of UCIRI and external affairs officer, Ixtepec, June 20, 1996.

9. Interview with Roberto Raygoza Beltran, Lachiviza, June 14, 1996.

10. Van der Hoff, Franz. *Organizar la Esperanza*, Ph.D. Thesis, Universidad Católica de Nimega. Kampen: Uitgeversmaatschappij J. H. Kok, 1992.

Chapter 6
Consumer Power

ORIGINS OF THE FAIR-TRADE MOVEMENT

Awareness of the rights and responsibilities of consumers began to gather momentum during the 1960s, when a young lawyer named Ralph Nader won a battle with General Motors over their manufacturing of unsafe cars. More recently, consumers' concern over the social and environmental effects of various products has manifested itself in campaigns to persuade such companies as The Gap, Shell, Nike, the Disney Corporation and Starbucks to change their business practices.

Fair trade is part of this wave of interest in ethical consumption. It is difficult to pinpoint exactly when the fair-trade movement started: a number of initiatives seem to have begun at about the same time on several continents. In North America, the Mennonite International Development Agency (now known as the Mennonite Central Committee) instigated the first direct-purchasing project with impoverished Latin American craftspeople, as early as 1946. Their first stores, Self-Help Crafts (today known as Ten Thousand Villages), were opened by volunteers who wanted to educate their communities about the inequities of international commerce and the need to pay a fair price to producers. In

Europe, in 1950 Oxfam began planning sales of crafts made by Chinese refugees in its British stores, and soon afterwards a group of young Dutch activists started directly importing Haitian wood sculptures in order to help the craftspeople become economically independent.

Initially named alternative trade, the burgeoning movement originally was aimed not at reforming conventional trading practices, but rather at creating a parallel system that would open markets to disadvantaged Southern producers and craftspeople. The organizations involved in this movement wanted to build relationships based on justice, not charity, in order to put an end to exploitation. As one project followed another, the concept of alternative trade started to strengthen into what is now usually known as fair trade, with the organizations involved establishing a set of core principles that they strive to respect in their dealings with all their partners.

Specific criteria have been established by fair-trade certification organizations for different products such as coffee, tea, bananas, cocoa, etc. The certification process and rules for fairtrade coffee are set out in detail in the Appendixes. In general, however, a fair-trade product must be bought from democratically organized small-scale producers at a price that will provide them with a decent standard of living. The purchasing must be as direct as possible in order to prevent speculation and to cut out unnecessary intermediaries. Southern partners must have access to credit from their Northern counterparts and both parties must be encouraged to develop long-term relationships. Production techniques must be environmentally friendly and the producer organizations must be democratically managed.

A growing success story

Thanks to consumer support, fair-trade projects have sprung up on all continents. But although fair trade originated in North America, its greatest impact on consumers has been in Europe. In the case of coffee, between 75 and 80 percent of the world's certified fair-trade production is distributed in

European shops, offices, and restaurants.[1] Consumers in Switzerland, the Netherlands, Belgium and Germany can find fair-trade coffee in the stores of any nationwide grocery chain.[2] There are currently over 70,000 points of sale for fair-trade products in Europe. Besides coffee, they sell sugar, tea, bananas, spices and nuts, as well as a wide range of crafts: woven baskets, jewellery, clothing, ceramics, cards, and toys.[3] At the production end, fair trade benefits more than 800,000 producer families in the South—over 5 million people in 45 countries.[4]

Fair-trade organizations

Over the years, the fair-trade movement has achieved a considerable degree of organization and collaboration. Two important umbrella organizations are the International Federation for Alternative Trade (IFAT) and the European Fair Trade Association (EFTA), which bring together about a hundred fair-trade organizations (FTOs) from all over the world. Their main role is to facilitate the exchange of information on markets and sources for fair-trade products. They also lobby public institutions and attempt to raise public awareness of fair-trade issues.

An important role is played by independent certification organizations. As large numbers of new fair-trade products arrived on the market in the 1980s, it became vital to develop a method of guaranteeing that such products were in fact equitably traded, and that the production process complied with certain well-defined criteria. It all started with coffee.

The first fair-trade certification program began in 1988, in the Netherlands. The Max Havelaar Foundation was named after the hero of a Dutch novel who denounced the treatment of Indonesian coffee planters during the Dutch colonial period. By establishing a certification process, it was hoped that fair-trade coffee could be marketed more easily through conventional channels and thus reach a larger number of consumers. Several conventional coffee roasters warmed to the idea and soon began marketing Max Havelaar's certified fair-trade coffee. For the first time, certified fair-trade products could be found on the shelves of major supermarkets and in restaurants rather than only in the stores of nonprofit organizations and church groups.

After the Netherlands, certification was adopted in other European countries, then in North America and Asia. These initiatives have greatly increased fair-trade coffee sales. Many European countries now also certify fair-trade bananas, sugar, tea, chocolate, honey and orange juice. Although there is no independent certification process for crafts, the members of the International Federation of Alternative Trade share principles similar to those of certified fair trade.

FAIR-TRADE LABELS

TransFair, Max Havelaar and the Fair Trade Foundation are all international certification organizations which put their logo on fair-trade food products such as coffee, tea, cocoa, bananas, honey and sugar. Beyond simply respecting the certification criteria, companies must pay the certification organization a licence fee which, in the case of coffee, costs between about $0.18 and $0.29 per kg ($0.08 and $0.13 per lb.) depending on the country. This money finances the monitoring process and the promotion of the seal.[5] All these certification initiatives are united under the umbrella of Fairtrade Labelling Organizations International (FLO-International) which has been working to standardize the certification process since 1997.

TransFair

 In Canada and the USA, TransFair puts its label on certified fair-trade coffee. The same seal is used in Germany, Japan, Austria, Luxembourg and Italy. Although a recent addition to packages of North American coffees, this logo is sought after by a growing number of consumers.

In North America

	TransFair Canada	TransFair USA
Founded	1994	1995
Number of licensees (August 2001)	70	103
Amount of fair-trade coffee sold in 2000	191,000 kg (420,000 lb.)	1.95 million kg (4.3 million lb.)

Max Havelaar

 Since 1988, the Max Havelaar certification label has met with great success in Europe. In Holland, for example, 90 percent of consumers are familiar with this label. Over 130 brands of certified fair-trade coffee are sold at 35,000 outlets in Europe.[6] In Switzerland one can find Max Havelaar in the vast majority of grocery stores. Many European supermarkets have entire sections devoted to fair-trade coffee, tea, sugar, chocolate, bananas and other produce certified by Max Havelaar.

Fair Trade Foundation

 The Fair Trade Foundation is the fair-trade certification mark in Britain and Ireland. Fair-trade coffee is served in the British parliament and many government buildings, and is available in most supermarkets. The British government has strongly supported the fair-trade movement .

Source: Information sheet, Max Havelaar France, 1998

THE CERTIFICATION PROCESS FOR FAIR-TRADE COFFEE

Every player in the fair-trade chain has a role to play in abiding by the agreed rules of the game. The criteria decided upon by the certification organizations are applied in as fair a manner as possible, while accounting for cultural and economic differences that exist both in the North and in the South.

Inspectors visit Southern cooperatives every one to two years, depending on their volume of production and the needs of the producers. In May 2001, 363 producers' organizations from 22 countries were listed in the FLO's fair-trade registry. Of these, 110 have been only provisionally accepted and may be granted permanent status after two coffee seasons, once they have demonstrated an ability to honour their commercial agreements. The coops registered on the FLO list can be found in Bolivia, Brazil, Cameroon, Colombia, Costa Rica, the Democratic Republic of Congo, the Dominican Republic, El Salvador, Guatemala, Haiti, Honduras, Mexico, Nicaragua, Papua-New Guinea, Peru, Tanzania, Uganda, Ecuador, Venezuela, Ethiopia, Indonesia and Thailand.

As for the roasters, inspection procedures vary somewhat for each certification organization, usually depending on their financial resources. In Switzerland, visits are made every six to 12 months, whereas in Canada and in the USA such visits are less frequent. After these inspections, certifiers have the authority to revoke the licences of cooperatives and roasters that do not meet their criteria and have done so.

In contrast to organic certification, certification fees are paid by the roasters, rather than the producers. For a coffee to be certified fairly traded, it is not enough that its cooperative of origin be listed in FLO-International's Registry of Coffee Growers. The coffee's movements must also be strictly controlled, which is beyond the cooperatives' sphere of operation. Roasters must show their books and warehouses in order to assure certifiers that they too have complied with the rules of fair trade and are entitled to affix a fair-trade logo to their products when appropriate.

FLO-International criteria for fair-trade coffee are presented in the Appendix A, together with the organic guidelines of the International Federation of Organic Agriculture Movements (IFOAM) and the Conservation Coffee Principles and criteria for shade-grown coffee put together by the Consumer's Choice Council.

FAIR-TRADE COFFEE IN NORTH AMERICA

Thanks to a growing awareness of the injustice of our economic system, fair trade has begun to catch on quickly in North America during the last few years. Between 1998 and 2000, sales of fair-trade coffee quadrupled in Canada and multiplied 37-fold in the USA.[7] Today more than 60 roasters are offering over 200 different blends of fair-trade coffee across Canada. In the USA, the number of roasters has reached 100. The demand is growing every day to the point that the certification organizations are facing challenges posed by rapid growth.

The price of fair-trade coffee, like that of any other product, varies from one brand to another depending on the business practices and expenditures of the supplier. Product quality, salaries, rent, spending on marketing, profit margins, packaging, transportation and investors' returns are all covered in the price charged to consumers. Fair-trade products are not necessarily more expensive than regular market products of the same quality. In some cases they can be cheaper. Some fair-trade roasters claim that they are able to offer a cheaper product than conventional competitors at equivalent quality because buying directly from coops saves money by reducing the number of intermediaries. Others argue that trading directly is more complicated and time-consuming than dealing with brokers and thus entails higher costs, making their fair-trade coffee more expensive. A survey by the Specialty Coffee Association of America found that quality rather than price, customer demand, or convenience of supply was the overwhelming criterion for industry purchasing decisions regarding fair-trade, organic and shade-grown coffees.[8] Price is thus one factor among a number of others that influence the development of sustainable coffee.

Almost all the fair-trade coffee available in North America is gourmet coffee. Approximately 79 percent of it is certified organic.[9] In contrast with the situation of a few years ago, the majority of consumers can now find a variety of fair-trade blends to choose from in their area. The list of companies offering at least one fair-trade coffee is growing almost daily.

The companies presented below have built their businesses upon fair trade as a founding principle, and buy 100 percent of their green beans on fair-trade terms. By doing so, and at the same time succeeding as viable businesses, they are demonstrating to the coffee industry that fair trade could be the basis for *all* coffee trading. Like conventional firms, they operate in the black and cover their own costs, but unlike conventional firms they reject the idea that greater profits, growth and maximizing shareholder value must come first. For them profitability is more a means to continue their work than an end in itself.

Ten Thousand Villages

Shortly after World War II, the Mennonites of North America were the first to voice the concept of fair trade between rich and poor and put their ideas into action by setting up the first alternative-trade shops. Today, the nonprofit organization Ten Thousand Villages markets a wide range of fair-trade craft goods and some foodstuffs in some 200 stores across North America. Thousands of volunteers help in their home community. Some organize festivals to bring an international marketplace to any community in North America for a day or two at a time. This fair-trade organization has two goals: first, to support craftspeople and peasants in the South by securing a market for them; and second, to inform people in the North about international inequalities. Ten Thousand Villages works with people of all cultures and religions in more than 25 countries.

Equal Exchange

Equal Exchange was founded in Boston in 1986 with the purpose of creating a firm that could act as a role model for other businesses. Their aim has been to respect the needs of farmers, employees, consumers and the environment. They consider that they achieved their goals by being a worker-owned cooperative with an egalitarian pay scale, and through their 100 percent fair-trade policy and product line of affordable speciality-grade organic coffees and premium teas.

In 1991, after the collapse of the International Coffee Agreement that had maintained world coffee prices, Equal Exchange looked to Europe and adopted the international standards for fair trade. No certification system existed in the US in 1991, and for years Equal Exchange was the only significant North American supplier of fair-trade coffee.

Beyond pioneering fair trade in the US coffee market, Equal Exchange has spent years fine-tuning its system for providing affordable credit to farmer coops, which it sees as fundamental to the fair-trade ethos, even though this ties up considerable capital, and is not practised by most other coffee importers. Equal Exchange helped provide over $440,000 in low-cost credit to partners in 2001.

Equal Exchange trades directly with 17 different small-farmer coffee cooperatives in 10 countries. Routine visits to the coops and the fact that they have worked with some partners for 10 or more consecutive years has led to very close relationships. At the other end of the coffee chain, they have a growing outreach and public-education program with faith-based organizations such as Lutheran World Relief, the American Friends Service Committee and the Presbyterian Church-USA.

After starting small they now import approximately 680,000 kg (1. 5 million lb.) annually. But because of the current record low prices in the coffee market, in 2001 Equal Exchange paid over $800,000 in above-market fair-trade premiums (more than 10 percent of their total annual revenue of $7.8 million).

Equal Exchange has been buying coffee from UCIRI since 1989 and uses their beans in its "Mind, Body and Soul" and "Organic Mexican" coffees, and "Organic French Roast" blends. Equal Exchange also buys from other coops in Southern Mexico: CEPCO, CIRSA, and Sierra de Motozintla.

Just Us!

When Jeff and Deborah Moore found themselves out of work in 1995, they decided they wanted to set up their own business—but not just any business.[10] Jeff and Deborah had long been sensitive to international-development issues, having worked in Latin America and having been involved in social-justice causes. After coming across a special issue of *New Internationalist* magazine devoted to fair-trade coffee, they dreamed of setting up one of Canada's first fair-trade coffee roasting companies.

Jeff was already passionate about coffee, but at that time, there was little information or assistance available to help him connect with fair-trade cooperatives. He had to go to Mexico to make his first link. In Chiapas, he went to La Selva where he found an impressive organization with great coffee. However, the bad news was that from the coop's perspective, in view of the logistics of processing, shipping and keeping the coffee safe from bandits, it did not make sense to export less than a full container of coffee: 17 tonnes, valued at $60,000. Such a purchase required Jeff and Deborah to use their house as collateral to secure financing, without having a single customer. That risk gave birth to the Just Us! coffee-roasting company of Nova Scotia.

Demand for their products was strong and in less than six months they were sold out. Just Us! then diversified its sources of supply and now purchases coffee from other cooperatives, most of which also have organic certification, in Mexico, Costa Rica, Peru and Guatemala. Just Us! distributes fair-trade coffee to more than 50 points of sale in the Maritime provinces of Canada, including the supermarket chains Coop Atlantic, Sobeys and Loblaws Super Stores. Sales for the year 2000 exceeded CDN$1 million. Since the company is a worker-owned coop, profits are ploughed back into the organization to help develop new projects. Today, Just Us! products have expanded to include fair-trade tea, chocolate and crafts, with clothing just around the corner.

Café Rico

In the autumn of 1997, Guylaine Bombardier first read about fair-trade coffee in an article published in the Montréal weekly paper *Voir*. It was a review of the book *Une cause café*—the first edition of the book that you are now reading. She was moved to learn of the exploitation of coffee farmers and inspired by the potential of consumer power to make a difference after visiting the nonprofit organization A SEED (today Équiterre), which was launching its *A Just Coffee* campaign to promote fair trade in Québec. She and her husband Stéphane Tamar Kordahi then travelled to Central America, and spent three weeks at the Costa Rican coffee cooperative, Coocafé, living with coffee farmers, learning about their situation and understanding how fair trade operated at the producers' end.

Back in Montréal, Stéphane decided to leave his job as a broker in asset management and make fair trade his everyday work. At that time the only fair-trade coffee available in Québec was imported from the USA and from Nova Scotia. With enormous energy, he developed a business plan and found premises where he could not only roast and serve fair-trade coffee, but also create a social space where progressive ideas could spread through photo exhibitions, book launches and other events. Café Rico opened in February 1999 and quickly became a great success, for the quality of the products as much as for the ideals behind them. Stéphane and Guylaine proved to all the sceptics that fair-trade principles were not merely utopian, but could serve as the foundation for a sustainable business.

Café Rico has since joined Café Campesino and eight other Canadian and American roasters to form a green-coffee importing cooperative. Though this group, Cooperative Coffees, they have united efforts to facilitate not only direct imports of coffee but also special partnership with fair-trade and organic coops in Costa Rica, Guatemala, Nicaragua and Mexico.

In 2000, Café Rico sold 13,500 kg (29,000 lb.) of coffee from its premises and through a dozen stores and restaurants in Québec. Stéphane prepares seven blends of coffee from seven countries. Although opportunities to expand his business through various projects, such as franchises, have been presented to him, he prefers a "think small" approach. He believes in quality and in the strength of a variety of players who share the same principles rather than in the establishment of a huge business. He has inspired and helped other businesses to become involved in fair trade. Today he is exploring new fair-trade projects such as direct importing of cocoa and mango vinegar in order to help the coffee coops he works with to diversify.

WHEN THE BIG BOYS MOVE IN: MULTINATIONAL CORPORATIONS IN THE FAIR-TRADE MOVEMENT

In recent years, North American sales of fair-trade coffee have boomed and some big players have contributed to this. What was originally the province of a few small roasters has been adopted by multinationals such as Starbucks, Sara Lee and Van Houtte. Like smaller companies, they have signed licensee agreements with Transfair and have committed themselves to abiding by the criteria of fair trade for a certain amount of their coffee. Their wide distribution network has made fair-trade coffee much more widely available across North America—Starbucks alone has over 2,300 stores across the USA.

The involvement of such big names is unquestionably very good news for thousands of small coffee farmers. But the fact that big corporations are eligible to use the fair-trade seal has raised questions in the minds of some activists and long-established fair-trade coffee roasters. They wonder why small-scale production and democratic principles of organization should be criteria for coffee growers but not for roasters. What does "fair" mean—and fair for whom? On this point, opinions are numerous.

What should be recognized is that, generally speaking, the rich countries where fair-trade coffee is being bought have stronger labour regulations and better social safety nets than most of the countries where coffee is grown. Exploitative working conditions and poverty are much more visible in coffee-growing areas than in richer countries. The coffee industry can no longer ignore the plight of small coffee growers, especially now that farmers are facing severe economic hardships as a result of the catastrophic slump in prices on the New York and London coffee markets. The consequences of "unfair trade" are borne by those who pick the coffee more than anyone else. This is undeniable. The coffee industry is starting to wake up to its own unsustainability.[11]

In practice, the extent of the commitment by some companies is questionable. Some roasters appear to be using fair trade to shield themselves against criticism from consumers and are making little effort to promote their fair-trade brands. Some appear to have adopted fair-trade coffee in order not to lose customers rather than as a means of assuming their responsibility towards coffee farmers. They talk about it as a new trend, like flavoured coffees. Some retailers show a serious lack of information in answering questions about fair trade, which does not help its development.

However, despite the fact that some businesses seem to be using fair trade to protect or enhance their public image rather than out of a real commitment, it must be acknowledged that this is a first step in a positive direction. It is then up to us consumers to keep on the pressure every time we have the chance. We need to make sure that the coffee we choose wears the fair-trade certification logo. We can decide whether to buy it from a small local company or a bigger one. The more people buy fair-trade coffee, the sooner it will become a must for all businesses, large and small.

CAMPAIGNING FOR FAIR TRADE

All over the developed world, men and women of all ages and all walks of life are coming together to raise awareness of fair trade and pushing to make fairly traded products more accessible to consumers—as individuals simply asking for fair-trade coffee in restaurants and stores, or as groups of volunteers armed with various tools. Organizations such as Équiterre, Global Exchange, the Canadian Council for International Cooperation, Ten Days for Global Justice and Oxfam have organized very effective campaigns to make people realize the political power of their consumer choices.

Internationally, Oxfam has been leading the way in promoting fair trade for over 40 years. Oxfam-UK alone currently works with over 160 producer organizations in some 30 countries around the world. In Belgium, the popular "world shops" selling fair-trade products arose out of the Oxfam movement. Over the last 10 years, Oxfam International has increased its campaigning and lobbying activities denouncing the negative social and environmental effects of the dominant trading system. It publishes and distributes well-researched policy papers and raises consumer awareness of the issues of ethical trade and child labour.[12]

In Canada, Équiterre has developed many education-for-action tools aimed at creating a snowball effect for fair trade. The organization has mobilized groups across Québec and Canada which have used Équiterre's material to build their own local campaigns. A variety of public-information activities have been organized and an information kit put together to encourage businesses to make fair-trade coffee more accessible. Équiterre has aroused the interest of the media, organized slide-show lecture tours, staged a photo exhibition, and has organized debates, street theatre, and letter-writing campaigns, with a view to moving both consumers and retailers into fair trade.

Rather than initiating a boycott to put pressure on coffee companies, Équiterre (like Transfair Canada and other groups) has chosen another strategy: so-called "buycotting" campaigns. These encourage consumers to ask for fair-trade coffee and buy it where available, to prove to corporations that the public is interested in fair-trade products, thereby creating a demand.

This was the strategy behind the postcard campaign directed at Paul-André Guillotte, head of Van Houtte, one of the largest players in the Canadian coffee industry. As you can see on page 59, Van Houtte owns many brands and is especially strong in the office coffee-service market. After meetings with Équiterre representatives and after receiving thousands of postcards mailed by consumers over three years, the company finally signed on. The company is now offering one kind of fair-trade coffee through its organic line, "Les Amoureux du café." Many consumers are hoping for more choices, especially in view of the company's recent record profits—profits fuelled by the current low prices paid to producers on the conventional market.

In the USA, the nonprofit organization Global Exchange has put forward a more assertive strategy. Across the country, a network of activists, church groups, students, labour unions and environmentalists has been mobilized against sweatshop-style labour practices in coffee production. Global Exchange has targeted companies and organized protests in front of cafes. Starbucks was one of the first companies they approached. Deborah James, Fair Trade Director at Global Exchange, explains:

We chose Starbucks because it is the largest speciality coffee retailer, with one fifth of all cafes in the country. In the fall of 1999, Global Exchange approached then CEO Howard Schultz and requested that Starbucks offer fair-trade certified coffee in all its stores. The company was initially very hesitant, alleging the beans were of low quality. Shortly thereafter, we organized several peaceful demonstrations in front of Starbucks stores in Seattle.

In February 2000, an investigative report by San Francisco's ABC TV affiliate exposed child labour and scandalously low wages on Guatemalan coffee planta-tions, some of which sell coffee to Starbucks. Immediately after the program aired, we organized a local protest. We then petitioned Starbucks stockholders at their annual meeting in Seattle to offer fair-trade certified coffee. That same week, the company announced a one-time shipment of 34,000 kg (75,000 lb.) of fair-trade coffee. We responded that for a firm as big as Starbucks, this repre-sented a "Drop in the Cup"—an average of only about 14 kg (30 lb.) per store, and the coffee was not certified! We then circulated an open letter, signed by 84 student, envi-ronmental, church, and social-justice organizations, again asking Starbucks to pay farmers a living wage and offer their customers fair-trade certified coffee. We helped plan 30 demonstrations that were scheduled for April 13 across the country at Starbucks shops. Meanwhile, hun-dreds of people faxed letters to Starbucks from our web-site or sent postcards asking the giant retailer to pay farmers fair prices.

> *Three days before our scheduled demonstrations,*
> *Starbucks announced an agreement with TransFair USA to*
> *offer fair-trade certified coffee at all its stores nationwide,*
> *beginning October 2000. They will also be developing*
> *educational material and training for coffee-bar workers,*
> *so that millions of consumers can learn about fair trade.*
> *This is a huge victory for farmers, whose incomes will*
> *triple when they can sell their coffee at fair-trade prices.*
> *It is also an important win for the corporate-accountabil-*
> *ity movement. Starbucks' quick capitulation in the face of*
> *nationwide protest illustrates that grassroots organizing*
> *and education can indeed bring major results.*[13]

The success of this campaign is a clear illustration of the fact that, once organized, consumers have much more power over companies than they think. They are the *raison d'être* of all companies.[14] Without consumers, there is no business.

Confused? Choices in "sustainable" coffee

So there you are in the store, a concerned consumer looking for coffee whose production involves neither exploitation of workers nor environmental damage. You'll soon find that fair-trade coffee is not the only alternative bean on the block. Coffee may also be labelled "shade-grown," "organic," "bird-friendly" or "eco-friend-ly." "Green" corporate advertising can also cloud the issue further—and this is why third-party certification is necessary.

You may notice that some coffees are certified organic, shade-grown and fair-trade, while others meet one standard but not others. This means you may have to make judicious choices based on what is on offer and on your primary motivation in looking for "alternative" or "sustainable" coffee.

As you will see, the various labels each address the many ecological and humanitarian issues surrounding coffee production to different degrees. Another important question to ask is: How can we be sure that what we are buying lives up to the claims made for it?

With the exception of organic, use of these terms is not regulated by government bodies in North America. Products that have been labelled organic by a producer comply with certain standards that are maintained by a government agency at the provincial, State or federal level. However, criteria vary from one region to another. The Standards Council of Canada recently approved a Canadian national standard for organic agriculture, but has not yet created a system of independent verification. In the USA, a national standard was approved for use in 2000 and will come into effect late in 2001. The US National Standard is generally accepted by the organic industry but there are a few problems with implementation. So at present the best way to make sure that a product is organic is still to look for a certification seal.

The same applies to the other terms mentioned above. To be sure that a product is "fair-trade" or "shade-grown," you should look for the certification seal of an independent organization.

Organic

Organic certification started in the 1970s and is currently the most developed process. Globally the estimated growth rates of the organic market range between 20-30 percent annually.[15] Certified organic products are increasingly moving from their market niche to the mainstream in most industrial countries.[16]

While there are many organic-certification bodies all over the globe, the most important coordinating organization for organic agriculture is the International Federation of Organic Agriculture Movements (IFOAM). Based in Germany, this worldwide umbrella organization has 740 member organizations in 103 countries.[17] It also holds official consultative status with the United Nations.

IFOAM does not certify products, but rather accredits affiliated organizations that are in charge of certifying farms in various countries. IFOAM creates specific standards for land stewardship, including the regulation of cutting and burning, and in the case of coffee, the planting of shade trees and the composting of coffee-fruit pulp.[18] Their guidelines for coffee production can be found in the Appendix B. The accredited certification bodies use IFOAM's generic standards and flesh them out, adding more details to take into account conditions in specific regions.

To be certified organic, coffee must first have been grown without any prohibited chemical fertilizers and pesticides. Organic-certification organizations such as Naturland and OCIA insist on rigorous soil-conservation methods such as composting and terracing to prevent soil erosion and measures to protect watercourses from runoff. Most organic coffee trees are grown under the shade of other trees, but a high level of biodiversity is not a mandatory criterion for all organic-certification organizations.

Organic agriculture requires much more work of the producers: pest-control such as weeding is done by hand and organic fertilizers such as compost have to be prepared. In terms of social standards, although most organic coffee is grown on small-scale plantations and sold for a higher price than regular coffee, organic certification does not guarantee that the peasants have received a fair share, nor that farm workers have been paid adequately. IFOAM is currently in the process of developing more in-depth social standards to address these issues.

Bird-friendly, or shade-grown

Concern over loss of biodiversity and disappearance of bird habitat is at the origin of the "bird-friendly" or "shade-grown" seal. The Smithsonian Migratory Bird Center (SMBC) has developed criteria for this certification in collaboration with the Commission for Environmental Cooperation and other environmental organizations and academics. The SMBC's logo can be found on coffee grown in areas with high biological diversity and low chemical input, under the shade of natural forest vegetation or planted shade trees. So far, it has limited the use of the seal to organic coffees that also meet its shade criteria.

Recently the Consumer's Choice Council has coordinated

the development of a set of conservation principles for coffee production. Environmental organizations such as the SMBC, Conservation International and the Rainforest Alliance have worked together in order to consolidate initiatives under the umbrella of these principles. The conservation principles are set out in the Appendix C.

Eco-friendly

The Conservation Agriculture Network has developed the ECO-OK certification for coffee. The secretariat for this network is the Rainforest Alliance, an environmental group based in New York. The ECO-OK seal combines some environmental and humanitarian criteria. Coffee has to be grown under shade, and chemical pesticides and fertilizers, although permitted, have to be kept to a minimum and strictly managed. Fair treatment and good conditions for workers must be provided and growers must not burn fuelwood other than waste wood from the pruning of coffee trees. New farms must not be set up on cleared forest land and vegetation buffers must be used to mitigate the polluting effects of pulp runoff in rivers.

Eco-friendly coffee differs from fair-trade coffee in some important respects: it is not necessarily produced by cooperatives, because large plantations can be certified and no minimum price is guaranteed. In terms of environmental criteria, they are less strict than organic standards regarding chemical inputs but have the advantage of addressing some landscape and biodiversity issues.

The goal of the ECO-OK seal is to have an impact on the largest possible area of agricultural land in the species-rich tropics. Its strength is that it monitors both social and environmental aspects of coffee production, but its weakness is that its standards are less stringent than other seals such as organic and fair trade.

As you might conclude from reading this overview, the "best"—indeed the most "sustainable"—coffee would meet fair-trade, shade-grown and organic criteria. Fortunately, in response to consumer demand, such coffee is becoming more and more widely available, although it does not always wear three certification labels. Slowly the various actors along the coffee routes are realizing the need to bring the environmental and social components of various initiatives into line with each other.

It remains true that greater collaboration among the various players would facilitate the development of strategies to bring sustainable coffee into the mainstream market. Increased cooperation between the various initiatives could also help improve the certification process and reduce the costs of certification and awareness-raising activities. If it is to make a difference on the large scale, "sustainable coffee" should not just be an alternative, but a staple.

TRANSFERRING RESPONSIBILITY TO THE CONSUMER

Although more and more citizens may wish to make a political statement with their consumer choices, they need access to information in order to make judicious decisions. (They don't have time to read a book about everything they buy!)

In an ideal world, people would be able to learn about the environmental and social impacts of what they buy simply by reading product labels. These impacts would need to be adequately measured before we could properly judge and compare the product's "real value." Such a label might resemble the "nutritional content" labels found on many food items sold in North America, and ideally it would become mandatory to provide this information everywhere in the world. This is unlikely to happen in the near future, considering that most governments are refusing to insist on labelling genetically modified food and that the World Trade Organization is restricting eco-labelling schemes. The right to know what we buy is a new concept, and has a long way to go before being officially recognized.

Not only is the WTO failing to address the issue of sustainable trade, it could also threaten existing initiatives. Under the Technical Barriers to Trade (TBT) agreement, many environmental and social regulatory standards are obstacles to free trade.[19] Voluntary, nongovernmental eco-labelling schemes may be judged to discriminate against "like" products on the basis of how they are produced rather than what they are. This means that "fair-trade," "shade-grown" and even "organic" certification labels could be challenged in front of the secretive WTO ruling panel.

To avoid the threat of WTO action, the leading international standard-setting, accreditation and labelling organizations in social and environmental certification have united under the International Social and Environmental Accreditation and Labelling (ISEAL) Alliance. One of ISEAL's objectives is to gain international recognition and credibility for their programs in the eyes of intergovernmental trade bodies and in the international arena. Consequently, they are working to secure acceptance of their criteria as international standards in order to avoid their initiatives' being considered technical barriers to trade.[20] The organizations currently participating in ISEAL are: Fairtrade Labelling Organizations International (FLO), the Conservation Agriculture Network (CAN), the Forest Stewardship Council (FSC), the International Federation of Organic Agriculture Movements (IFOAM), the International Organic Accreditation Service (IOAS), the Marine Stewardship Council (MSC), and Social Accountability International (SAI).

At first sight, sustainable-trade initiatives might appear like David fighting Goliath. Free-trade policies are buttressed by WTO rules and other trade agreements. Citizens often find themselves disempowered in the face of such structures and left without much governmental support to respond to the environmental and social problems exacerbated by increased international trade. Slowly however, people all around the world are becoming organized to make their voices heard and to take action. Nongovernmental organizations (NGOs) are springing up around the globe to defend various issues. These groups encompass a wide range of viewpoints and plans for action, and each in its own way is seeking to influence the beliefs and behaviour of people throughout the world. Some promote human rights, others international cooperation, environmental action, and justice. Every initiative is important and many are complementary. The ethical consumer's choice movement is only one strategy among many, but one which we can practise in our day-to-day lives, by buying according to our values. Goliath is facing many Davids.

Notes

1. Interview with Mr. Hans Bolscher, Max Havelaar Netherlands. Utrech, May 26, 1998.
2. Waridel, Laure and Teitelbaum, Sara. Research Report *Fair Trade in Europe: Contributing to equitable commerce in Holland, Belgium, Switzerland, and France*. Montréal: Équiterre, 1999.
3. European Fair Trade Association (EFTA). *Fair trade in Europe: Facts and figures on the fair-trade sector in 16 European countries*. Maastricht: European Fair Trade Association, 1998.
4. Ibid.
5. Fair TradeMark Canada. Campaign Kit, 1996, 3.
6. Équiterre, "What is fair-trade coffee?" *Fair Trade: a growing trend in the coffee industry*. May, 2000.
7. Data obtained directly from TransFair Canada and TransFair USA. June 2001.
8. Giovannucci, Daniele. *Sustainable Coffee Survey of the North American Specialty Coffee Industry*. Conducted for the Summit Foundation, the Nature Conservancy, the North American Commission for Environmental Cooperation, the Specialty Coffee Association of America and the World Bank. May, 2001.
9. Ibid., 24.
10. Telephone interview with Deborah Moore, cofounder of Just Us!, November 9, 1999.
11. Participation in the SCAA Coffee Conference. San Francisco, April 14-18, 2001.
12. Oxfam-UK: www.oxfam.org.uk.
13. James, Deborah. "Justice and Java: Coffee in a Fair Trade Market." *North American Congress on Latin America*. Vol. 34, No. 2 (October 2000).
14. Seybold, Patricia B. *The Customer Revolution: How to thrive when customers are in control*. New York: Crown Business, 2001.
15. International Federation of Organic Agriculture Movements. *IFOAM position document on organic agriculture. Prepared for the FAO conference "Cultivating our Future."* Maastricht: IFOAM, September 12-17, 1999.
16. Dicum, Greg, and Nina Luttinger. *The Coffee Book: Anatomy of an indus-*

try from crop to the last drop. New York: The New Press, 1999. Also: Browne, A.W., P.J.C. Harris, A.H. Hofny-Collins, and R.R. Wallace. *Ethical Trading: Definition, Practice and Possible Links with Organic Agriculture.* The Natural Resources Policy and Advisory Department of the Department for International Development. 1998. 24.

17. IFOAM, op. cit.

18. McLean, Jennifer. *Merging Ecological and Social Criteria for Agriculture: The Case of Coffee.* M.S. Research Paper. University of Maryland, December 1997.

19. Shrybman, op. cit. 11.

20. Mallet, Patrick. *ISEAL Alliance Strategic Role: Background Paper.* Knowlesville: Falls Brook Centre, May 2001.

Conclusion
Holding up the Stream of Inequity

Coffee is brewing. As I start the day, the rich aroma fills my kitchen, like those of millions of others.

Sitting at my computer in my Montréal apartment, I think of Adela, Félix and all the people thanks to whom I can drink my coffee. As I write these lines, Adela has long finished making the tortillas for the day. Every morning she rises before the sun to start the cooking fire and claps between her hands a dough made from the corn they have grown. By now, Felix must be in the mountains weeding his small coffee plantation or sowing corn seeds. He has probably walked along the little path next to the river, greeting people on his way. In a plastic bottle, he carries very sweet coffee, boiled in a thin aluminum pan with more sugar than coffee. The best quality beans are exported. The worst are kept for family consumption.

Seen from outside, Adela and Felix's life seems to be an ideal of beauty. Surrounded by a cloud forest, they live in a wonderful environment where orchids grow wild and free. A place where wealthy people would pay big money to go on vacation. Yet, although the situation of many people in the village of Guadalupe has improved as a result of their involvement with the coffee cooperative UCIRI, there still have many worries. They are struggling for things most Northern coffee drinkers take for granted: basic social services, justice, respect and democracy. Native people and peasants are generally downtrodden in Mexico. The Zapatista rebellion which started in the neighbouring State of Chiapas has its roots in the subjugation of native people. The colonial conquest still reverberates throughout the country. Coffee cooperatives and fair trade have been an important empowering tool for thousands of small coffee farmers in Mexico and around the world, but have not solved all their problems.

The coffee crisis is affecting everyone in the mountains. No one can escape, especially those who are still selling their coffee to coyotes, at a cheaper price than ever. The low prices of coffee are triggering a rural exodus toward sweatshop zones and the USA.

The last time I left Guadalupe, I met a young man sitting next to me on the roof of the bus. With his little red bag, Arturo was starting his journey to the US border. His eyes were glowing with stories he had heard of and seen on TV. His uncle had been living in Los Angeles for years and regularly sent money back to the family. He would help him to find a job. Arturo had no papers. When I told him about the beauty of his village and my feeling for his people, he looked at me smiling. I could read in his eyes that it was easy for me to say that. I could come and go as I wish. My survival did not depend on the fertility of the land nor on the price of coffee. My political opinions did not put my life at risk. My skin was white, I had education and a Canadian passport.

The world is unfair and we all know it. What this book has tried to show is that we can make difference—a bigger one than we imagine. Every choice that we make has an impact on other people's lives and on the environment. We are perpetually connected with thousands of men, women and children who have grown the food that we eat, sewn the clothes that we wear, and produced everything around us. If we could only see them through the labels on these products, we would have another perspective. Coffee has a different taste for me, now that I know the work and the hopes behind it.

In rich countries we have become very good at talking about rights and liberties—especially our own. Responsibilities are another matter. It takes time to realize that by not taking our responsibilities towards others we are infringing on our own liberties.

I sometimes compare the state of our planet today to a city in the Middle Ages. At that time, people threw garbage and sewage out of the windows. They did not realize that they were poisoning themselves, contributing to the propagation of terrible infectious diseases. This behaviour was seen as normal until a few people started making the connection and pointed out the problem. To change people's habits took time and a complex process involving education, city planning and regulation.

In the same way, we are contaminating our own environment and society with what we consider "normal behaviour." But slowly, people are starting to make connections.

I remember a few years ago, after returning from my first trip to Mexico, trying to convince a coffee roaster of the importance of fair trade. He laughed, telling me that everyone was for virtue and justice, but that when the time came to put it into practice, the story was different. There is truth in what he said. As I pointed out in the Introduction, many of us are quick to condemn big corporations for being focused solely on profits, while congratulating ourselves on getting the cheapest deal.

But today that same coffee roaster's company is selling fair-trade coffee certified by Transfair Canada. This is not because of the conversation we had. What convinced him were the demands of his customers. Money talks.

By asking for fair-trade, organic and shade-grown coffee we create a demand that puts pressure on businesses. Coffee is simply an eye-opener, an example if what can happen for all products. We make the market: the global market. It is time to show that we want more than cheap products. Our choices can help build an economic system that serves people and not the other way around. The experience of fair trade and the impact it has had on people's lives shows that this is no mere pipe dream.

The globalization of social and environmental justice goes beyond words: daily actions are what gives it life. Just as democracy means more than going to vote once every few years. Democracy happens every day with what we say to politicians and businesses, with what we buy and how we behave towards people around us. Today's revolution, and the revolutions to come, start in our heads and take shape with in each of our daily actions. We can each add a small stone to the dam that will hold back the flow of injustice. All this to give to our society the humanity that we owe it, the humanity we all deserve.

Appendixes

Appendix A
Fair-Trade Certification Criteria for Coffee

Fairtrade Labelling Organizations International (FLO) coordinates the certification process for various fair-trade products. The structure of the organization as well as the certification criteria are currently being reviewed. Up-to-date information is available on the FLO web page at www.fairtrade.net. The current criteria for coffee follow.[1]

ELIGIBILITY CRITERIA FOR COFFEE GROWERS

To be included in FLO-International's Registry of Coffee Growers, applicants must conform to the following standards:

1. Small-scale production
The members of the group must themselves produce on a small scale. They must depend on the family for labour and not on external sources.

2. Democratic management
Members must participate in the decision-making process of their group. They decide what projects the group will undertake and what to do with the profits of fair trade.

3. Transparency
The board of directors, elected by the members, must ensure transparent operations in order to minimize the risk of fraud.

4. Values based upon solidarity
The motivation underlying the organization's existence must be the practice of solidarity. There can be no political, racial, religious, or sexual discrimination. The organization must be open to new members.

5. Political independence

The organization cannot be the instrument of a political party or another such political interest.

6. Sustainable development

The group shares the following values and objectives with FLO-International and the other members of the Registry of Coffee Growers:

- Use agricultural techniques that are environmentally friendly and contribute to the conservation of natural resources in an effort to prevent or eliminate the use of any chemical products.
- Favour an integrated economic-development strategy that seeks to improve production techniques, and diversification of production in order to reduce dependence upon a single product as the source of all income.
- Promote integrated social-development projects using a variety of means to improve the living conditions of members and the community as a whole. For example, such projects may focus on personal hygiene, housing conditions, education, clean water supply, or any matters that the members identify as an important need in the community.
- Improve production quality so that the group can develop its market within the conventional network, in addition to the fair-trade network.

NORTH-SOUTH ELIGIBILITY CRITERIA

Producers, importers, roasters, and wholesalers must meet the following standards in order to be granted a fair-trade certification label:

1. Direct trade

All green coffee destined to carry a fair-trade logo must be bought directly from a cooperative listed in FLO-International's Registry of Coffee Growers. Some 363 producer organizations from 22 countries are currently listed in the registry. Of these, 110 have only been provisionally accepted and may eventually attain permanent status once they have demonstrated an ability to honour their commercial agreements for at least two harvests.[2]

2. A long-term relationship

Buyers and sellers must agree to a long-term and stable relationship in which the rights and interests of both parties are mutually respected. No agreement is permitted that describes a period less than one full harvest cycle. All long-term agreements are confirmed by an exchange of letters of intent, in which both parties agree upon the conditions of sale: volumes, qualities, method of determining the final price, and the dates for sending the final product. The parties must reach an agreement, confirmed by letter of intent, for each contract, before the harvest begins.

3. Higher than market prices

Purchasing prices must reflect certain conditions set by FLO-International, including:

Base price
- For Arabica, New York's "C" Market is the base indicator. The price is stated in US$ per lb., adding or subtracting the difference according to the FOB indicator, the country of origin, and net weight transported.
- For Robusta, London's "Fox" Market is the base indicator. The price is stated in US$ per tonne, adding or subtracting the difference according to the FOB indicator, the country of origin, and net weight transported.

Premiums
- In addition to the base price, there is an additional $0.11 per kg ($0.05 per lb.) if free-market prices rise above the fair-trade set price.
- Organic coffee must have an officially recognized certification. An additional $0.33 per kg ($0.15 per lb.) of green coffee is added above the price set by FLO-International.
- Minimum prices vary according to the coffee's country of origin. The minimum prices are listed below: they account for differences in quality, the premium of $0.11 per kg ($0.05 per lb.) set by FLO-International, and the $0.33 kg ($0.15 per lb.) premium for certified organic products.

FAIR-TRADE COFFEE

	Conventional production		Certified organic production	
	Central America/ Mexico/Africa	South America/ Caribbean	Central America/ Mexico/Africa	South America/ Caribbean
Washed Arabica	1.26	1.24	1.41	1.39
Unwashed Arabica	1.20	1.20	1.35	1.35
Washed Robusta	1.10	1.10	1.25	1.25
Unwashed Robusta	1.06	1.06	1.21	1.21

Prices in US$ per pound, FOB port of origin

4. Access to credit

At the seller's request, the importer must make available a line of credit up to 60 percent of the original contract, based on the minimum price laid down by FLO-International. The seller and purchaser agree upon an interest rate that cannot be higher than those present in Europe at the time of the agreement, which are considerably lower than those currently found in Latin America and Africa. The line of credit is terminated once the coffee has been shipped.

THE ROLE OF CERTIFIERS

The certification organizations, which are members of FLO-International, must ensure that their production and marketing criteria are clearly respected by all participants. The Registry of Coffee Growers is administered by a committee elected from among the members of FLO-International. All importers and roasters must sign a licensing contract with the FLO-International member organization in their country of origin. Responsibility for ensuring that criteria are respected by the cooperatives as far as the borders of the importing country lies with FLO-International. Once the coffee reaches the national market, the local certification organization is responsible as far as the store shelf or until the coffee is distributed elsewhere.[3] In summary, FLO-International is responsible for:

1. Listing producer-group members in FLO-International's Registry of Coffee Growers. Maintaining clear lines of communication with these producers and assisting them as far as possible in their development. Ensuring that the producers respect all fair-trade criteria.

2. Guaranteeing the fair-trade status of a given product by ensuring the continuous inspection and control of all roasters selling coffee bearing the TransFair, Max Havelaar or FairTrade logos.

3. Informing and educating consumers, and promoting the sale of fair-trade coffee.

Notes

1. FairTrade Labelling Organizations International. *Les conditions pour l'achat de café Max Havelaar/TransFair/FairTrade.* Utrecht: FairTrade Labelling Organizations International, June 1995. 9. Also: www.fairtrade.net.
2. Information from Bob Thomson, Director of FairTrade Mark Canada, Ottawa, November 18, 1998.
3. De Cenival, Laure. *Commerce équitable, citoyenneté d'entreprise et des consommateurs.* Paris: Solagral/FNDVA, 1997.

Appendix B
Organic Coffee Certification

INTERNATIONAL FEDERATION OF ORGANIC AGRICULTURE MOVEMENTS (IFOAM)

Numerous organic-certification bodies exist over the globe. However, many of them operate under the umbrella of the International Federation of Organic Agriculture Movements (IFOAM). Based in Germany, this world-wide organization brings together over 700 member organizations in more than 100 countries. IFOAM itself does not certify products but rather accredits affiliated organizations that are in charge of certifying farms in various countries. They make sure that the IFOAM standards are respected. IFOAM is registered by the ISO as the international standard-setting body for organic agriculture.

The accreditation service of IFOAM is organized in a separate but closely linked organization in the USA: International Organic Accreditation Services (IOAS). Unlike IFOAM, this body does not include producer representation, leaving IFOAM as the standard-setting and rule-making body.

In order to be recognized as organic by an IFOAM-accredited certification body, coffee has to respect IFOAM's general organic standards as well as the specific criteria for coffee developed by the certification body itself.

The current IFOAM accredited certifiers are: KRAV (Sweden), National Association for Sustainable Agriculture (Australia), Farm Verified Organic (USA), Instituto Biodinamico (Brazil), Bioagricoop (Italy), Naturland (Germany), California Certified Organic Farmers (USA), Organic Growers and Buyers Association (USA), Argencert SRL (Argentina), Bio-Gro (New Zealand), Boilcert (Bolivia), Soil Association Certification Ltd. (United Kingdom), Agrior Ltd (Israel),

Organizacion Internacional Agropecuaria S.A. (Argentina), AIAB (Italy), CCPB (Italy), and Ekoagros (Lithuania). The following organizations are applicants: OIA (Argentina), ACT (Thailand), JONA (Japan), Bioland (Germany), Organic Farmers & Growers Ltd. (United Kingdom), Organic Food Development Center (P.R. China), Quality Assurance International (USA), KEZ (Czech Republic), Biological Farmers of Australia (Australia), and Biopark e.V. (Germany).

IFOAM standards are evolving over time to further contribute to the development of organic farming throughout the world. The entire IFOAM Basic Standards for Organic Production and Processing are available on IFOAM's web page (www.ifoam.org).* The extracts presented below have been selected from this very complete document touching on all aspects of organic certification from production to processing and labelling. Only the principles, recommendations and standards most relevant to coffee production have been selected.

SECTION B
GENERAL PRINCIPLES, RECOMMENDATIONS AND STANDARDS

1. The principal aims of organic production and processing

Organic production and processing is based on a number of principles and ideas. They are all important and are not necessarily listed here in order of importance.

- To produce food of high quality in sufficient quantity.
- To interact in a constructive and life-enhancing way with natural systems and cycles.
- To consider the wider social and ecological impact of the organic production and processing system.
- To encourage and enhance biological cycles within the farming system, involving microorganisms, soil flora and fauna, plants and animals.
- To develop a valuable and sustainable aquatic ecosystem.
- To maintain and increase long-term fertility of soils.
- To maintain the genetic diversity of the production system and its surroundings, including the protection of plant and wildlife habitats.
- To promote the healthy use and proper care of water, water resources and all life therein.
- To use, as far as possible, renewable resources in locally organized production systems.

---

* *IFOAM General Assembly in Basel, Switzerland, September 2000.*

- To create a harmonious balance between crop production and animal husbandry.
- To give all livestock conditions of life with due consideration for the basic aspects of their innate behaviour.
- To minimize all forms of pollution.
- To process organic products using renewable resources.
- To produce fully biodegradable organic products.
- To produce textiles which are long-lasting and of good quality.
- To allow everyone involved in organic production and processing a quality of life which meets their basic needs and allows an adequate return and satisfaction from their work, including a safe working environment.
- To progress toward an entire production, processing and distribution chain which is both socially just and ecologically responsible.

2. Genetic engineering
General principles
Genetic engineering has no place in organic production and processing.

Standards
2.1. Certification bodies/standardizing organizations shall set standards and make every effort, including relevant documentation, to ensure that no genetically engineered organisms or products thereof are used in organic production and processing.
[For a definition of genetic engineering, see the IFOAM glossary on p. 137.]

(...)

4. Crop production
4.1. Choice of crops and varieties
General principles
All seeds and plant material should be certified organic.

Recommendations
Species and varieties cultivated should be adapted to the soil and climatic conditions and be resistant to pests and diseases.
In the choice of varieties genetic diversity should be taken into consideration.

Standards

4.1.1. When organic seed and plant materials are available, they shall be used. The certification body/ standardizing organization shall set time limits for the requirement of certified organic seed and other plant material.

4.1.2. When certified organic seed and plant materials are not available, chemically untreated conventional materials shall be used.

Where no other alternatives are available chemically treated seed and plant material may be used. The certification body/ standardizing organization shall define conditions for exemptions and set time limits for any use of chemically treated seeds and plant materials.

4.1.3. The use of genetically engineered seeds, pollen, transgenic plants or plant material is not allowed.

4.2. Length of conversion period

General principles

The establishment of an organic management system and building of soil fertility requires an interim period, the conversion period. The conversion period may not always be of sufficient duration to improve soil fertility and reestablish the balance of the ecosystem but it is the period in which all the actions required to reach these goals are started.

Recommendations

The length of the conversion period must be adapted to:
- the past use of the land
- the ecological situation

Standards

4.2.1. Plant products from annual production can be certified organic when the standards requirements have been met for a minimum of twelve months before the start of the production cycle. Perennial plants (excluding pastures and meadows) can be certified organic at the first harvest after at least eighteen months of management according to the Standards requirements. Pastures, meadows and their products can be certified after 12 months of organic management.

Where the certification body/ standardizing organization requires a period of three or more years of documented non-use of prohibited materials, certification may be granted twelve months after application.

4.2.2. The conversion period can be extended by the certification body/ standardizing organization depending on, for example, past use of the land and environmental conditions.

4.2.3. The certification body/ standardizing organization may allow plant products to be sold as "produce of organic agriculture in process of conversion" or a similar description, when the Standards requirements have been met for at least twelve months.

4.3. Diversity in crop production
General principles
The basis for crop production in gardening, farming and forestry is consideration of the structure and fertility of the soil and surrounding ecosystem and to provide a diversity of species while minimizing nutrient losses.

Recommendations
Diversity in crop production is achieved by a combination of:
- a versatile crop rotation including legumes
- an appropriate coverage of the soil for as much of the year as possible with diverse plant species

Standards
4.3.1. Where appropriate, the certification body/ standardizing organization shall require that sufficient diversity is obtained in time or place in a manner that takes into account pressure from insects, weeds, diseases and other pests, while maintaining or increasing soil organic matter, fertility, microbial activity and general soil health. For non-perennial crops, this is normally, but not exclusively, achieved by means of crop rotation.

4.4. Fertilization policy
General principles
Sufficient quantities of biodegradable material of microbial, plant or animal origin should be returned to the soil to increase or at least maintain its fertility and the biological activity within it.

Biodegradable material of microbial, plant or animal origin produced on organic farms should form the basis of the fertilization program.

Recommendations
- Fertilization management should minimize nutrient losses.
- Accumulation of heavy metals and other pollutants should be prevented.
- Nonsynthetic mineral fertilizers and brought-in fertilizers of biological origin should be regarded as supplementary and not a replacement for nutrient recycling.
- Adequate pH levels should be maintained in the soil.

Standards

4.4.1. Biodegradable material of microbial, plant or animal origin shall form the basis of the fertilization program.

4.4.2. The certification body/ standardizing organization shall set limitations to the total amount of biodegradable material of microbial, plant or animal origin brought onto the farm unit, taking into account local conditions and the specific nature of the crops.

4.4.3. The certification body/ standardizing organization shall set standards which prevent animal runs from becoming overmanured where there is a risk of pollution.

4.4.4. Brought-in material shall be in accordance with Appendices 1 and 2.

4.4.5. Manures containing human excrement (feces and urine) shall not be used on vegetation for human consumption, except where all sanitation requirements are met. The certification body/ standardizing organization shall establish sanitation requirements and procedures shall be in place which prevent transmission of pests, parasites and infectious agents.

4.4.6. Mineral fertilizers shall only be used in a supplementary role to carbon-based materials. Allowance for use shall only be given when other fertility-management practices have been used.

4.4.7. Mineral fertilizers shall be applied in their natural composition and shall not be rendered more soluble by chemical treatment.

The certification body/ standardizing organization may grant exceptions which shall be well justified. These exceptions shall not include mineral fertilizers containing nitrogen.

4.4.8. The certification body/ standardizing organization shall lay down restrictions for the use of inputs such as mineral potassium, magnesium fertilizers, trace elements, manures and fertilizers with a relatively high-heavy metal content and/or other unwanted substances, e.g. basic slag, rock phosphate and sewage sludge (Appendices 1 and 2).

4.4.9. Chilean nitrate and all synthetic nitrogenous fertilizers, including urea, are prohibited.

4.5. Pest, disease and weed management including growth regulators
General principles
Organic farming systems should be carried out in a way which ensures that losses from pests, diseases and weeds are minimized. Emphasis is placed on the use of crops and varieties well-adapted to the environment, a balanced fertilization program, fertile soils of high biological activity, adapted rotations, companion planting, green manures, etc.

Growth and development should take place in a natural manner.

Recommendations
Weeds, pests and diseases should be managed by a number of preventive cultural techniques which limit their development, e.g. suitable rotations, green manures, a balanced fertilization program, early and predrilling seedbed preparations, mulching, mechanical control and the disturbance of pest-development cycles.

The natural enemies of pests and diseases should be protected and encouraged through proper habitat management of hedges, nesting sites, etc.

Pest management should be regulated by understanding and disrupting the ecological needs of the pests.

Standards
4.5.1. Products used for pest, disease and weed management, prepared at the farm from local plants, animals and microorganisms, are allowed. If the ecosystem or the quality of organic products might be jeopardized, the Procedure to Evaluate Additional Inputs to Organic Agriculture (Appendix 3) and other relevant criteria shall be used to judge if the product is acceptable. Brand name products must always be evaluated.

4.5.2. Thermic weed control and physical methods for pest, disease and weed management are permitted.

4.5.3. Thermic sterilization of soils to combat pests and diseases is restricted to circumstances where a proper rotation or renewal of soil cannot take place. Permission may only be given by the certification body on a case-by-case basis.
4.5.4. All equipment from conventional farming systems shall be properly cleaned and free from residues before being used on organically managed areas.

4.5.5. The use of synthetic pesticides is prohibited. Permitted products for plant-pest and disease control, weed management and plant growth regulators may be found in Appendix 2.

4.5.6. The use of synthetic growth regulators is prohibited. Synthetic dyes may not be used for cosmetic alteration of organic products.

4.5.7. The use of genetically engineered organisms or products thereof is prohibited.

4.6. Contamination control
General principles
All relevant measures should be taken to minimize contamination from outside and within the farm.

Recommendations
In case of risk or reasonable suspicion of risk of pollution, the certification body/ standardizing organization should set limits for the maximum application levels of heavy metals and other pollutants.

Accumulation of heavy metals and other pollutants should be limited.

Standards
4.6.1. In case of reasonable suspicion of contamination the certification body shall make sure that an analysis of the relevant products and possible sources of pollution (soil, water, air and inputs) shall take place to determine the level of contamination and take measures accordingly.

4.6.2. For protected structure coverings, plastic mulches, fleeces, insect netting and silage wrapping, only products based on polyethylene and polypropylene or other polycarbonates are allowed. These shall be removed from the soil after use and shall not be burned on the farmland. The use of polychloride-based products is prohibited.

4.7. Soil and water conservation
General principles
Soil and water resources should be handled in a sustainable manner.

Recommendations
Relevant measures should be taken to prevent erosion, salination of soil, excessive and improper use of water and the pollution of ground and surface water.

Standards
4.7.1. Clearing of land through the means of burning organic matter, e.g. slash-and burn or straw burning, shall be restricted to the minimum.

4.7.2. The clearing of primary forest is prohibited.

4.7.3. Relevant measures shall be taken to prevent erosion.

4.7.4. Excessive exploitation and depletion of water resources are not allowed.

4.7.5. The certification body shall require appropriate stocking rates which do not lead to land degradation and pollution of ground and surface water.

4.7.6. Relevant measures shall be taken to prevent salination of soil and water.

(...)

IFOAM GLOSSARY

Additive: An enrichment, supplement or other substance which may be added to a foodstuff to affect its keeping quality, consistency, colour, taste, smell or other technical property (for a full definition, see the Codex Alimentarius).

Ayurvedic: Traditional Indian medicine.

Breeding: Selection of plants or animals to reproduce and / or to further develop desired characteristics in succeeding generations.

Buffer zone: A clearly defined and identifiable boundary area bordering an organic production site that is established to limit application of, or contact with, prohibited substances from an adjacent area.

Certification: The procedure by which an independent third party gives written assurance that a clearly identified production or processing system is methodically assessed and conforms to specified requirements.

Certification mark: A certification body's sign, symbol or logo which identifies product(s) as being certified according to that program's standards.

Certification program: System operated by a certification body with its own rules, procedures and management for carrying out certification of conformity.

Conventional: Conventional means any material, production or processing practice that is not certified organic or organic "in-conversion."

Crop rotation: The practice of alternating the species or families of annual and/or biennial crops grown on a specific field in a planned pattern or sequence so as to break weed, pest and disease cycles and to improve soil fertility and organic matter content.

Genetic engineering: Genetic engineering is a set of techniques from molecular biology (such as recombinant DNA) by which the genetic material of plants, animals, microorganisms, cells and other biological units may be altered in ways or with results that could not be obtained by methods of natural reproduction or natural recombination.

Green manure: A crop that is incorporated into the soil for the purpose of soil improvement.

Homeopathic treatment: Treatment of disease based on administration of remedies prepared through dilution and succession of a substance that in larger amounts produces symptoms in healthy animals similar to those of the disease itself.

IFOAM accreditation: Recognition by the International Organic Accreditation Service that a certification body is complying with the IFOAM Basic Standards and IFOAM Accreditation Criteria.

Ingredient: Any substance, including a food additive, used in the manufacture or preparation of a food or present in the final product although possibly in a modified form.

Irradiation (ionizing radiation): High-energy emissions from radio nucleotides, capable of altering a food's molecular structure for the purpose of controlling microbial contaminants, pathogens, parasites and pests in food, preserving food or inhibiting physiological processes such as sprouting or ripening.

Labelling: Any written, printed or graphic representation that is present on the label of a product, accompanies the product, or is displayed near the product.

Natural fibres: A filament of plant or animal origin that is not synthetic.

Organic: "Organic" refers to the farming system and products described in these standards and not to "organic chemistry."

Organic product: A product which has been produced, processed, and/or handled in compliance with organic standards.

Parallel production: A producer, handler, or processor that grows, breeds, raises, handles, or processes a given product as certified organic and as otherwise. This includes (a) as nonorganic (b) in conversion or (c) organic but not certified.

Processing aid: Any substance or material, not including apparatus or utensils, and not consumed as a food ingredient by itself, intentionally used in the processing of raw materials, foods or its ingredients, to fulfil a certain technological purpose during treatment or processing and which may result in the nonintentional but unavoidable presence of residues or derivatives in the final product.

Appendix C
Shade-grown Coffee for Biodiversity Conservation

The Consumer's Choice Council (CCC), in collaboration with the Rainforest Alliance, the Smithsonian Migratory Bird Center, Conservation International, and the Summit Foundation has coordinated the development of a set of Conservation Principles for Coffee Production. This initiative is a first step to strengthen the shade-grown coffee movement, which is mainly established in the USA. It hopes to promote greater clarity as well as opportunities for collaboration around the issue of coffee. The final version of the Conservation Principles for Coffee Production is presented below. More information can be found on the CCC web page: www.consumerscouncil.org. Other organizations involved with conservation coffee initiatives are also listed at the end of this book.

CONSERVATION PRINCIPLES FOR COFFEE PRODUCTION

Final version, 25 May 2001

Coffee farming is an economic mainstay in the world economy. It is the primary source of income for millions of farmers across the tropical world and even for entire countries, where coffee provides the primary source of foreign-exchange earnings. Coffee production also overlaps with many of the biologically richest regions of the world and can contribute both to their endangerment and to their protection. Given the right conditions, coffee production can be both economically and ecologically beneficial.

However, the world coffee industry is in crisis. Current prices are lower than the costs of production in many parts of the world, and there is little expectation that this will change in the short term. Coffee farmers the world over, most of whom are small-scale producers already living in poor conditions, are experiencing a substantial decline in their meagre incomes. In some countries, extensive areas of tropical forest are being converted to coffee fields, compounding low-quality production, global overproduction and biodiversity loss. Chronic low prices undermine the capacity of farmers to produce a quality product and maintain its value, to protect their farms and natural resources, and to sustain their very livelihoods. This situation has the potential to become a social and environmental disaster on a world scale.

In the last two decades, a sustainable-coffee movement has emerged that tries to create alternative market opportunities that pay farmers decent prices, provide incentives for organic production and reward farmers for practising good stewardship of their natural resources. While this movement has made great strides in increasing awareness of these issues among policy makers, businesses, producers and consumers alike, there remains an enormous gap between what a market for sustainable coffee could provide for the world and the present conditions of the world coffee market. The progress that has been achieved by the sustainable-coffee movement could be undone by the continued depression of prices paid to producers.

In order to help strengthen the sustainable-coffee movement, and to promote greater clarity and opportunities for collaboration around the specific issue of conservation in the world coffee industry, the Consumer's Choice Council has coordinated the development of a set of Conservation Principles for Coffee Production. Patrick Mallet of Falls Brook Centre crafted this document in collaboration with Conservation International, Rainforest Alliance, and the Smithsonian Migratory Bird Center, with funding from the Summit Foundation.

These principles were developed with several goals in mind:

• **Align coffee production with biodiversity conservation:** A clear and concise set of Conservation Principles for Coffee Production can help guide strategies to improve coffee production and conserve biodiversity. The Principles can also help identify where additional scientific information and technical solutions are needed to address the environmental complexities of coffee production and trade flows around the world.

- Create tools and incentives that promote and reward good stewardship in the coffee industry: The Conservation Principles for Coffee
Production can serve as a valuable reference point for producers, importers,
exporters, roasters and consumers who are working to incorporate conservation into management and purchasing decisions. They can strengthen the
market profile for responsible coffee through incorporation into existing certification programs, and so create market opportunities that acknowledge
and reward good stewardship.

- Strengthen collaboration and facilitate local standards development:
The Conservation Principles for Coffee Production provide a conservation
baseline for coffee production around which businesses, certification agencies, producer associations, development agencies and other interested parties may collaborate to address conservation issues more efficiently and with
greater effect. They can help strengthen existing conservation initiatives and
provide a catalyst for new initiatives, while providing a foundation for developing conservation standards tailored to local environments.

- Inform planning and monitoring: The Principles can help guide ecological
landscape planning, environmental-impact assessment, farm-management
plans, monitoring and record keeping, as well as other tools essential for
implementing and verifying agro-ecological improvements in worldwide coffee production. All applications of the Principles should strive for trans-
parency, accountability and maintain rigorous documentation to substantiate
claims of conservation benefit.

- Influence public policy and financing: The Principles can influence the
development of pro-conservation policies, programs and extension services
by national governments and international institutions. Priorities within conservation policy should include effective protected area programs and environmental regulation, as well as avoiding incentives for conversion of coffee
plantations to full sun cultivation or for expansion of coffee production into
new areas at the expense of natural forest.

Conservation Principles for Coffee Production

The following Conservation Principles for Coffee Production apply to farms and processing facilities in all coffee-growing regions of the world and should be the foundation of any conservation-based certification program. In addition, they can be used to guide the development of industry sourcing guidelines and codes of conduct, changes in government or financial-sector policy to encourage sustainable agriculture, and modernization of technical assistance programs. It is also recognized that coffee quality is fundamental to market value. A complementary emphasis is required through all stages of the coffee value chain to ensure delivery to the consumer of a high-quality product

In many cases, these Principles require collaboration between producers, communities and local and national governments. Specific applications of these Conservation Principles will vary by region in accordance with their climates, ecological variables, traditions and cultures. However, programs that aim to improve coffee-production systems must at least address and monitor progress in accordance with the following Conservation Principles to ensure that there is a real conservation benefit.

1. Sustainable livelihoods: Coffee-production systems and commercialization should improve the social and economic livelihoods of producers and provide economic benefits to local communities.
- Coffee producers are empowered to access markets and to develop long-term trading relationships with buyers.
- Equitable prices for producers are a primary consideration in all marketing agreements.
- Coffee producers are encouraged to diversify their sources of income through the development of on-farm and/or community-based alternatives to coffee production.
- Coffee producers should apply long-term management plans that guide farm production activities and that are periodically revised to address the environmental and social impacts of production, as determined by ongoing monitoring and audits.
- Communities are directly involved, from the beginning, in a participatory process of management planning, monitoring and implementation.
- Cooperatives work to ensure that the basic rights and needs of their members are met and are committed to continual improvement over time.
- Coffee farms that employ workers conform to local laws and applicable inter-

national conventions related to workers' rights and benefits and are in a process of continual improvement over time.
· Wages and benefits meet or exceed the minimum required under local and national laws.
· Working conditions meet or exceed applicable laws and regulations related to health and safety of workers.
· Workers and their families, including seasonal workers, are provided with access to potable water, sanitary facilities, adequate housing, education and training, transportation, and health services.
· Workers' rights to organize and negotiate freely with their employers are guaranteed in accordance with local laws and international obligations.

2. Ecosystem and wildlife conservation: Coffee-production systems maintain and enhance biological diversity and ecosystem functions on farms and surrounding areas.
· There is no disturbance of intact natural forest.
· Rare, threatened or endangered species and habitats are protected, including adequate measures to restrict hunting and commercial collection of threatened flora and fauna.
· Where coffee is grown in areas originally covered by forest, a canopy cover of diverse native tree species that conserves local and endemic biodiversity is incorporated into coffee-production systems.
· Pruning of shade trees preserves their reproductive processes and protects the habitat they provide for plants and animals.
· Areas of high ecological value located on and around coffee farms and producer communities, including wetlands and native forests, are protected.
· Coffee farms and surrounding areas create a diverse landscape mosaic that serves as wildlife habitat and migration corridors between protected areas.
· Land restoration programs using native species are implemented on areas degraded by unsustainable cropping, grazing or extractive practices.

3. Soil conservation: Farm-management practices control erosion and conserve or enhance soil structure and fertility.
· Most soil nutrients are supplied by on-farm sources, by means such as organic fertilizers, cover crops, mulch and compost.
· Environmentally appropriate measures are taken to control erosion and build soil quality, particularly on sloped terrain or adjacent to water courses and wetland areas.

4. Water conservation and protection: Coffee-production systems reduce water use to the greatest extent possible and prevent pollution of all water sources.

- All existing sources of contamination are eliminated and potential sources are managed, to prevent pollution of water resources.
- Vegetative buffer zones are in place adjacent to all water sources.
- The volume of water used in wet processing and on farms is continually reduced through the application of more efficient technologies and recycling of water.
- No alteration of the course or hydrology of streams or other surface water occurs.

5. Energy conservation: Energy is used efficiently at all stages of the coffee-production system, and renewable sources of energy are used whenever possible.

- Efforts are made to reduce the use of nonrenewable energy sources such as petroleum-based fuels and to incorporate renewable sources of energy such as solar drying.
- Firewood comes from well-managed sources that avoid degradation of natural forest and that employ environmental safeguards.

6. Waste management: Waste and coffee by-products are managed to minimize environmental impacts by applying the principles of reduction, reuse and recycling.

- Measures are taken to continually reduce the overall quantity of waste produced on the farm.
- All organic farm by-products and domestic waste, including coffee pulp and parchment, are composted and reused in the coffee-production system.
- Recycling of inorganic waste is encouraged. Inorganic waste that is not recycled, including chemicals and other toxic materials, is not burned and is properly managed, using landfills if available.

7. Pest and disease management: Coffee-production systems strive to eliminate all inputs of chemical pesticides, fungicides, herbicides and synthetic fertilizers.

- Farms are certified organic or are demonstrating increasing reductions in the toxicity and quantity of synthetic agrochemicals being applied, leading to the elimination of agrochemical use.

- Organic management techniques are employed, including biological, cultural and mechanical pest and disease controls. Monitoring programs are in place to assist in the application of non-chemical preventive controls.
- Synthetic agrochemicals are used only in extreme cases when necessary to avert severe crop loss and substantial economic failure.
- No agrochemicals that are banned for agricultural use in their country of use, country of origin or by international agreement are stored or used on the farm.
- Effective measures are taken to ensure the health and safety of farm workers who may handle or be exposed to agrochemicals, including the provision of education, protective clothing and access to adequate medical treatment.
- All farm inputs are applied in a selective, targeted manner in order to minimize drift to neighboring fields, polluted run-off or groundwater contamination.

CCC Glossary

Agrochemicals: Synthetic substances used to control competition from other organisms (e.g. pesticides and herbicides), and to provide crops with the nutrients necessary to compensate for lack of soil fertility (fertilizers).

Areas of high ecological value : Those areas that possess one or more of the following attributes:
- areas containing globally, regionally or nationally significant concentrations of biodiversity;
- areas that are in or contain rare, threatened or endangered ecosystems;
- areas that provide basic services of nature (e.g. watershed protection or erosion control) in critical situations;
- areas fundamental to meeting the basic needs of local communities (e.g. subsistence or health)
- areas critical to local communities' traditional cultural identity (areas of significance identified in cooperation with such local communities).

Biological diversity: The variability among living organisms from all sources including, inter alia, terrestrial, marine and other aquatic ecosystems and the ecological complexes of which they are a part; this includes diversity within species, between species and of ecosystems.

Buffer zones: In protecting critical ecological areas, the buffer is an area of forest land that reduces the impacts of adjacent activities on the critical area. In managing biosphere reserves, it is a portion or edge of a protected area that has land-use controls that only allow activities compatible with the objectives of the protected area.

Canopy cover: The multiple storeys of foliage in a stand of trees or shrubs, in particular the uppermost continuous layer of branches and foliage.

Degraded land: Land that has suffered damage to its natural composition, structures and functions to such an extent that the structures required for future ecological processes are no longer present.

Economic failure: In the context of this document, a substantial loss of crops due to factors external to the management practices of the farm, resulting in severe negative economic repercussions and potential bankruptcy to the farm or cooperative.

Ecosystem: A community of plants, animals, and their physical environments, functioning together as an interdependent unit.

Endangered species: Any species which is in danger of extinction throughout all or a significant portion of its range.

Landscape mosaic: The pattern of different ages and types of ecosystems distributed across the landscape.

Local laws: Includes all legal norms given by organisms of government whose jurisdiction is less than the national level, such as departmental and municipal laws, as well as customary norms.

Long-term: The time-scale manifested by the objectives of the management plan and the commitment to maintain a viable ecological system. The length of time will vary according to ecological conditions, and will be a function of how long it takes a given ecosystem to recover its natural structure and composition following disturbance.

Natural: Areas where many of the principal characteristics and key elements of native ecosystems such as complexity, structure and diversity are present.

Organic: An integrated system of farming based on ecological principles, that replenishes and maintains long-term soil fertility by optimizing conditions for biological activity within the soil, rather than through the application of agrochemicals.

Renewable sources of energy: Any resource that provides energy and is capable of indefinite renewal on a human-based time scale.

Restoration: A process of returning ecosystems or habitats to their native structure and species composition.

Threatened species: Any species that is endangered or is likely to become endangered within the foreseeable future throughout all or a significant portion of its range.

Appendix D
Moving into Action: Contact Lists

People are organizing to raise awareness of fair trade and pushing to make the products of this type of exchange more accessible to consumers. Other are promoting shade-grown and organic coffee—and very often all of the above! Groups of volunteers have organized information kiosks, slide-show presentations, letter-writing sessions and massive postcard campaigns to request sustainable coffee from large corporations. Organizations such as Équiterre and Global Exchange, and many others listed below, have produced material that will help you get involved. Much of it is on the Web. Or, you can simply ask the person who sells you coffee to make it fair and environmentally friendly. Businesses are sensitive to consumer demands. People do not need to be experts to know what they want.

Organizations involved with fair-trade coffee
Also see the list of fair-trade certification bodies presented on page 154

International

International Federation for Alternative Trade (IFAT)
30 Murdock Road
Bicester, Oxon OX6 7RF
Britain
Tel.: 44 1869 249 819
Fax: 44 1869 246 381
Email: cwills@ifat.org.uk
www.ifat.org

Network of European World Shops (NEWS)
Coordination Office
Catharijnesingel 82,
Utrecht 3511 GP
Netherlands
Tel.: 31 30 230 0820
Fax: 31 30 230 0440
Email: eunexs@worldline.nl
www.worldshops.org

**European Fair Trade Association
(EFTA)**
Advocacy & Campaigns Office
c/o Maison Internationale
139, Rue Haute,
B-1000 Brussels
Belgium
Tel.: 32 2 213 12 46
Fax: 32 2 213 12 51
Email: efta@eftadvocacy.org
www.eftadvocacy.org

Head Office
Boschstraat 45
NL-6211 AT Maastricht
Netherlands
Tel.: 31 43 3256917
Fax: 31 43 3258433
Email: efta@antenna.nl
www.efta.org

Austria
Arge Weltläden
Viehgatter 23
A-6800 Feldkirch
Tel.: 43 5522 78079
Fax: 43 5522 78079
Email: arge.weltlaeden@aon.at
www.weltlaeden.at

Belgium
Magasins du monde-Oxfam
7a, rue Michiels
B-1180 Bruxelles
Tel.: 32 2 3320110
Fax: 32 2 3321888
Email: mdm.oxfam@skynet.be
www.mdmoxfam.be

Oxfam Wereldwinkels
Ververystraat 15-17
B-9000 Gent
Tel.: 32 9 2188899
Fax: 32 9 2188877
Email: oxfam.wereldwinkels@oww.be
www.oww.be

Canada
**Canadian Council for
International Cooperation**
1 Nicholas Street, suite 300
Ottawa, ON, K1N 7B7
Tel.: 613 241-7007
Fax: 613 241-5302
Email: ccic@ccic.ca
www.fly.web.net/ccic-ccci
www.incommon.web.net/

Équiterre (formerly A SEED)
2177, Masson, suite 317
Montréal, QC, H2H 1B1
Tel.: 514 522-2000
Fax: 514 522-1227
Email: info@equiterre.qc.ca
www.equiterre.qc.ca

Oxfam Canada
National Office
300, 294 Albert St.
Ottawa, ON, K1P 6E6
Tel.: 613 237-5236
Fax: 613 237-0524
Email: infoott.oxfam.ca
www.oxfam.ca

Oxfam Québec
2330, rue Notre-Dame Ouest,
Bureau 200
Montréal, QC, H3J 2Y2
Tel.: 514 925-6001
Fax: 514 937-6720
Email: info@oxfam.qc.ca
www.oxfam.qc.ca

Ten Days for Global Justice
947 Queen St. East, Suite 201
Toronto, ON, M4M 1J9
Tel.: 416 463-5312
Fax: 416 463-5569
Email: tendays@web.net
www.web.net/~tendays

Ten Thousand Villages Canada
65 Heritage Drive
Box 869
New Hamburg, ON, N0B 2G0
Tel.: 519 662-1879
Fax: 519 662-3755
Email: inquiry@villages.ca
www.villages.ca

Denmark
U-Landsimporten
Rolstrupbkken 6
DK-7900 Nykobing Mors
Tel.: 45 97 725788
Fax: 45 97 725354
Email: handel@u-landsimporten.dk

Finland
Reilun kaupan edistämisyhditysry
Siltasaarenkatu 15
00530 Helsinki
Tel.: 358 9 7268 6630
Fax: 358 9 7262 102
Email: reilukauppa@reilukauppa.fi
www.reilukauppa.fi

France
Artisans du monde
3, rue Bouvier
F-75009 Paris
Tel.: 33 1 4372 3737
Fax: 33 1 4372 3637
Email: artisans-du-monde@globenet.org
www.globenet.org/artisans-du-monde

Germany
Gepa
Gewerbepark Wagner
Bruch 4, D-42279 Wuppertal
Tel.: 49 202 266830
Fax: 49 202 266831
Email: gf@gepa.org
www.gepa3.de

Ireland
Association of Fair Trade Shops in Ireland
c/o World Development Centre
3 Vulcan Street
Waterfort
Tel.: 353 51 873064
Fax: 353 51 873979
Email: wdcentre@tinet.ie

Oxfam Ireland
52-54 Dublin Road
Belfast, BT2 7HN
Tel.: 44 28 9023 0220
Fax: 44 28 9023 7771
Email: info@oxfamni.org.uk
www.oxfammireland.org

Italy
Associazione Botteghe del Mondo
Via Ferrari Bonini n.3
1-42100 Reggio Emilia
Tel.: 39 0522 541914
Fax: 33 0522 541914
Email: assobdm@tin.it
www.assobdm.it

Netherlands
Fair Trade Organisatie
Beesdweweg 5
P.O. Box 115
NL-4100 AC Culemborg
Tel.: 31 345 545151
Fax: 31 345 521423
Email: post@fairtrade.nl
www.fairtrade.nl

Landelijke Vereniging van Wereldwinkels
Catherijnesingel 82
NL-3511 GP Utrecht
Netherlands
Tel.: 31 30 2316312
Fax: 31 30 2300440
www.wereldwinkelsneek.myweb.nl

NOVIB (Oxfam Netherlands)
P.O. Box 30919
2500 GX The Hague
Mauritskade 9
2514 HD The Hague
Netherlands
Tel.: 31 70 342 1777
Fax: 31 70 361 4461
Email: info@novib.nl
www.novib.nl

Spain
IDEA
Avda. de Amargacena
Polígono Industrial Amargacena,
Parcela 9-Nave 7
14013 Córdoba
Tel.: 34 957 294805
Fax: 34 957 296974
Email: ideas-co@eurosur.org
www.eurosur.org/_ideas-co

Solidaridad Internacional
Marqués de Urquiijo 41, 1 Ext.
28008 Madrid
Tel.: 34 91 5413737
Fax: 34 91 5414343
Email: solint@ran.es
www.solidaridad.org

Sweden
Alternativ Handel
Heurlins Plants 1
S-41301 Gothenburg
Tel.: 46 31 7017600
Fax.: 46 31 7017601
Email: info@alternativhandel.com
www.alternativehandel.com

Switzerland
Association romade des magasins du monde
Rue de Genève, 52
CH-1004 Lausanne
Tel.: 41 21 6612700
Fax: 41 21 6612220
Email: asro-mdm@span.ch

Claro AG
P.O. Box 129
Byfangstraasse 19
CH-2552 Orpund
Tel.: 41 32 356 0700
Fax: 41 32 356 0701
Email: mail@claro.ch
www.claro.ch

United Kingdom
British Association for Fair Trade Shops (BAFTS)
c/o Gateway World Shop
Market Place
Durham DH1 4ED
Tel.: 44 191 3847173
Fax: 44 191 3750729
Email: info@classicfm.net

Cafédirect
66 Clifton Street
London EC 2A 4HB
Tel.: 44 20 7422 0730
Fax: 44 20 7422 0731
Email: info@cafedirect.co.uk
www.cafedirect.co.uk

Oxfam Fair Trade
274 Banbury Road
Oxford, OX2 7DZ
Tel.: 44 1865 315 903
Fax.: 44 1865 31 5909
Email: fairtrad@oxfam.org.uk
www.oxfam.org.uk

Twin Trading
3rd Floor, 1 Curtain Rd
London, EC2A 3LT
Tel.: 44 20 7375 1221
Fax: 44 20 7375 1337
Email: info@twin.org.uk
www.twin.org.uk

United States

Aid to Artisans
14 Brick Walk Lane
Farmington, CT 06032
Tel.: 860 677-1649
Fax: 860 676-2170
Email: atausa@aol.com
www.aid2artisans.org

Crafts Centre
1001 Connecticut Avenue NW
Washington, DC 20036
Tel.: 202 728-9603
Fax: 202 296-2452
Email: craftsdc@erols.com
www.craftscenter.org

Fair Trade Federation
1612 K Street, Suite 600
Washington, DC 20006
Tel .: 202 872-5329
Fax: 202 822-8471
Email: ftf@fairtradefederation.org
www.fairtradefederation.org

Fair Trade Resource Network
c/o Traditions Fair Trade
300 5th Ave. SW
Olympia, WA 98501
Tel.: 360 705-2819
Fax: 360 705-0747
Email: dick@traditionsfairtrade.com
www.fairtraderesource.org

Global Exchange
2017 Mission Str.303
San Francisco, CA 94110
Tel.: 415 255-7296
Fax: 415 255-7498
Email: fairtrade@globalexchange.org
www.globalexchange.org

Institute for Agriculture and Trade Policy (IATP)
2105, First Avenue South
Minneapolis, MN 55404
USA
Tel: 612 870-0453
Fax: 612 870-4846
Email: iatp@iatp.org
www.iatp.org

Lutheran World Relief
700 Light St. South
Baltimore, MD 21230
Tel.: 410 230-2700 /
(800) LWR-LWR2
Fax: 410 230-2882
Email: lwr@lwr.org
www.lwr.org

Oxfam America
26 West Street, Boston, MA 02111
Tel.: 617 728-2437
Fax: 617 728-2596
Email: lbrody@oxfamamerica.org
www.oxfamamerica.org

Ten Thousand Villages USA
704 Main Str.
PO Box 500
Akron, PA 17501-0500
Tel.: 717 859-8100
Fax: 717 859-2622
Email: inquiry@villages.mcc.org
www.villages.ca

Some organizations involved with organic and or shade-grown coffee

Bio-Gro New Zealand
PO Box 9693, Marion Square,
Wellington, 6031
New Zealand
Tel.: 64 4801 9741
Fax: 64 4801 9742
Email: emcmillan@bio-gro.co.nz
www.biogro.co.nz

**Certificadora Mexicana de
Productos y Procesos Ecológicos
S.C. (Certimex)**
Av. H. Escuela Naval Militar 621-301
Colonia Reforma
C.P. 68050
Oaxaca, Oaxaca
Mexico
Tel./Fax: 52 9 513-1196
Email: certimexsc@prodigy.net.mx

**Commission for Environmental
Cooperation (CEC)**
393, rue St-Jacques Ouest, Suite 200
Montréal, QC, H2Y 1N9
Canada
Tel.: 514 350-4340
Fax: 514 350-4314
Email: info@ccemtl.org
www.cec.org

Conservation International
1919, M Street NW, Suite 600
Washington, DC 20036
USA
Tel.: 202 912-1000
Fax: 202 912-1030
Email: info@conservation.org
www.conservation.org

Consumer's Choice Council (CCC)
2000 P Street, NY, Suite 540
Washington, DC 20036
USA
Tel.: 202 785-1950
Fax: 202 452-9640
Email: consumer@attglobal.net
www.consumerscouncil.org

ECO-OK
Rainforest Alliance
65 Bleecker St., 6th Floor
New York, NY 10012
USA
Tel.: 212 677-1900
Fax: 202 677-2187
eco-ok@ra.org
www.rainforest-alliance.org

**Instituto para el Desarollo
Sustentable en Mesoamérica
(IDESMAC)**
Avenida Cristobal Colón #35-B
El Cerrillo
San Cristobal de las Casas, Chiapas
México
Tel.: 52 9 678-2163
Fax: 52 9 678-4463
Email: idsmac@mundomaya.com.mx

**International Federation of
Organic Agriculture Movement
(IFOAM)**
Head Office
66636 Tholey-Theley
Germany
Tel.: 49 6853 919890
Fax: 49 6853 919899
headoffice@ifoam.org
www.ifoam.org

Naturland
Head Office
Kleinhaderner Weg, 182166,
Gräfelfing
Germany
Tel.: 49 89 8980820
Fax: 49 8989 808290
Email: argencert@interline.com.ar
www.naturland.de

**Organic Crop Improvement
Association (OCIA)**
1001 Y Street, Suite B,
Lincoln, NE 58508
USA
Tel.: 402 477-2323
Fax: 402 477-4325
Email: info@ocia.org
www.ocia.org

Pronatura Chiapas
Avenida Benito Juárez 11-B
Apartado Postal 219, Col. Centro
San Cristobal de las Casas
Mexico
Tel.: 52 9 678 5000
Fax: 52 9 678 5000
Email: imeldasolis@hotmail.com

Quality Assurance International
12526 High Bluff Drive, Suite 30
San Diego, CA 92130
USA
Tel.: 858 792 3531
Fax: 858 792 8665
Email.: quicert@cts.com

Seattle Audubon Society
8050, 35th Avenue NE
Seattle, WA 98115
USA
Tel.: 206 706-7827
Fax: 206 528-7779
Email: coffee@seattleaudubon.org
www.seattleaudubon.org/coffee

**Smithsonian Migratory Bird
Center**
National Zoological Park
Washington, D.C. 20008
USA
Tel.: 202 673-4908
Fax: 202 673-4916
Email: goughg@nzp.si.eu
www.natzoo.si.ed/smbc

**TerraChoice Environmental
Services**
2781 Lancaster Road, Suite 400
Ottawa, ON, K1B 1A7
Canada
Tel.: 613 247-1900
Fax: 613 247-2228
Email.: ecoinfo@terrachoice.ca
www.terrachoice.ca

Appendix D
Where to Get Fair-Trade Coffee

Many companies throughout the world have taken the fair-trade route. They have undertaken to comply with the principles of fair trade and have a certification licence. The Transfair, Max Havelaar and Fair Trade Foundation logos guarantee consumers that the coffee meets fair-trade criteria and that it has been subjected to an independent monitoring process. As a result, fair-trade coffee to suit all tastes can be bought from many different companies from one end of the continent to the other. A list of fair-trade coffee importers and roasters is available via the national fair trade certification organizations presented below. Many of them have this information posted on their web page.

Fair-trade certification bodies

Fairtrade Labelling Organizations International (FLO)

FLO International Secretariat
Poppelsdorfer Allee 17
53155 Bonn
Germany
Tel.: 49 228 94 92 30
Fax: 49 228 24 21 713
Email: coordination@fairtrade.net
www.transfair.net

FLO head office for coffee certification
Postbus 1252
3500 BG Utrecht
Netherlands
Tel.: 31 30 233 46 02
Fax: 31 30 2332 992
Email: motz@maxhavelaar.nl
www.transfair.net

TransFair Austria
Wipplingerstr. 32
A-1010 Wien
Austria
Tel.: 43 1 5330956
Fax: 43 1 5330957
Email: transfair.a@magnet.at
www.transfair.or.at

Max Havelaar France
41, Rue Emile Zola
F-93100 Montreuil
France
Tel.: 33 1 42877021
Fax: 33 1 48700768
Email: info@maxhavelaarfrance.org
www.maxhavelaarfrance.org

Max Havelaar Belgium
Aalstraat 7/11
B-1000 Brussels
Belgium
Tel.:32 2 213 36 20
Fax: 32 2 213 36 21
Email info@maxhavelaar.be
www.maxhavelaar.be

TransFair Germany
Remigiusstr. 21
50937 Köln
Germany
Tel.: 49 221 942040 0
Fax: 49 221 94204040
Email: info@transfair.org
www.transfair.org

Transfair Canada
323 Chapel Street, 2nd floor
Ottawa, ON K1N 7Z2
Canada
Tel.: 613 563-3351/1 888 663-3247
Fax: 613 237-5969
Email: fairtrade@transfair.ca
www.transfair.ca

Fairtrade Foundation
16 Baldwins Gardens, Suite 204
London EC1N 7RJ
Great Britain
Tel.: 44 207 405 5942
Fax: 44 207 405 5943
Email: mail@fairtrade.org.uk
www.fairtrade.org.uk

Max Havelaar Fonden Denmark
c/o FKN, Nørregade 13 kld
DK-1165 København
Denmark
Tel.:45 33 11 1345
Fax: 45 33 11 1347
Email: info@maxhavelaar.dk
www.maxhavelaar.dk

TransFair Italy
Passaggio De Gasperi 3
35131 Padova
Italy
Tel.: 39 049 8750 823
Fax: 39 049 8750 910
Email: transfai@intercity.it
www.citinv.it/equo/homefair.htm

Fairtrade Mark Ireland
Carmichael Centre
North Brunswick Street
Dublin 7
Tel.: 353 1 475 3515
Fax: 353 1 475 3515
Email: info@fair-mark.org
www.fair-mark.org

Max Havelaar Norge
Storgata 11
0155 Oslo
Norway
Tel.: 47 23 010330
Fax: 47 23 010331
Email: maxhavelaar@maxhavelaar.no
www.maxhavelaar.no

TransFair Japan
c/o St. Paul Lutheran Church of the
JELC
5-3-1 Koutoubashi, Sumida-ku
Tokyo 130
Japan
Tel.: 81 3 36347867
Fax: 81 3 36347808
Email: transfair@wakachiai.com
www.transfair-jp.com

**Reilun kaupan edistämisyhdistys
ry.** (Associate Member)
Siltasaarenkatu 15
00530 Helsinki
Finland
Tel.: 358 9 72686630
Fax: 358 9 7262102
Email: reilukauppa@reilukauppa.fi
www.reilukauppa.fi

TransFair Minka Luxemburg
13, Rue de la Gare
L-5353 Oetrange
Luxemburg
Tel.: 352 350762
Fax: 352 26350112
Email: transfai@pt.lu

Föreningen för Rättvisemärkt
Drakenbergsgatan 11
SE-117 41 Stockholm
Sweden
Tel.: 46 8 668 0350
Fax: 46 8 668 0314
Email: handla@raettvist.se
www.raettvist.se

Max Havelaar Netherland
Postbus 1252
3500 BG Utrecht
Netherlands
Tel.: 31 30 2334602
Fax: 31 30 2332992
Email: maxhavelaar@maxhavelaar.nl
www.maxhavelaar.nl

Max Havelaar Switzerland
Malzgasse 25
4052 Basel
Switzerland
Tel.: 41 61 2717500
Fax: 41 61 2717562
Email: postmaster@maxhavelaar.ch
www.maxhavelaar.ch

TransFair USA
(Associate Member)
52 Ninth Street
Oakland CA 94607
USA
Tel.: 510 663 5260
Fax: 510 663 5264
Email: transfair@transfairusa.org
www.transfairusa.org

Bibliography

- Adbusters. Corporate Spotlight. *Adbusters* (Vancouver). No. 34 (March-April 2001): 38.
- Barlow, Maude, and Tony Clark. *Global Showdown: How the New Activists Are Fighting Global Corporate Rule.* Toronto: Stoddart, 2001.
- Bartra, Armando. "El México Bárbaro: Plantaciones Y Monterías Del Sureste Durante El Porfiriato." Mexico City: El Atajo Ediciónes, 1996.
- Barrat-Brown, Michael. *Fair Trade.* London and New Jersey: Zed Books, 1993.
- Boudansky, Daniel. "The Legitimacy of International Governance: A Coming Challenge for International Environmental Law." *American Journal of International Law.* Vol. 93, No. 3. (July 1999).
- British Department for International Development. *Developments.* The International Development Magazine (London). No. 2, Second Quarter: 1998.
- Brière, Julie and Françoise Ruby. "Le top 10 des résidus de pesticides:" *Protégez-vous* (Montréal). (August 1995).18.
- Browne, A.W., P.J.C. Harris, A.H. Hofny-Collins, and R.R. Wallace. *Ethical Trading: Definition, Practice and Possible Links with Organic Agriculture.* The Natural Resources Policy and Advisory Department of the Department For International Development, 1998.
- Canadian International Development Agency (CIDA). *Mini-dictionary of International Development.* Ottawa: Supply and Services Canada, 1990.
- Cerny, Philip G. "Globalization and the Erosion of Democracy." *European Journal of Political Research* (Dordrecht). Vol. 36 (1999): 1-26.
- Chevalier, Jacques M., and Daniel Buckles. *A Land Without Gods.* London and New Jersey: Zed Books, 1995.
- Cohn, H. Theodore. *The International Politics of Agricultural Trade.* Vancouver: University of British Columbia Press, 1990.
- Collier, George A. *Basta! Land and the Zapatista Rebellion in Chiapas.* Oakland: Food First Book, 1994.
- Commission for Environmental Cooperation. *Measuring Consumer Interest in Mexican Shade-grown Coffee: An Assesment of the Canadian, Mexican and US Markets.* Montréal: Commission for Environmental Cooperation, 1999.

- Coote, Belinda. *The Trade Trap: Poverty and the Global Commodity Markets.* Oxford: Oxfam, 1992.
- Corporate Europe Observatory. *Europe, Inc.: Dangerous liaisons between EU institutions and industry.* Amsterdam: Corporate Europe Observatory, 1997.
- Courville, Sasha Leigh. *Not Just Trade: Steps Toward Incorporating Social and Ecological Costs into International Trade. Lessons Learned from 'Better' Case Studies of Coffee Production-to-Consumption Systems.* A thesis submitted for the degree of Doctor of Philosophy of the Australian National University. June 2001. 439.
- Courville, Sasha Leigh. *Promoting Biological Diversity Through Sustainable Certification and Fair Trade.* Minneapolis: Institute for Agriculture and Trade Policy, 1999.
- Cruz, Manuel Angel Gómez, Rita Schwentesius Rinderman, and Laura Gómez Tovar. "Agricultura Organica de México: Datos Basicos." Chapingo: Centro de Investigaciones Económicas, Sociales y Tecnológicas de la Agroindustria y la Agricultura Mundial, 2000.
- Daly, Herman E., and B. Coob Jr. *For the Common Good: Redirecting the economy toward community, the environment, and a sustainable future.* Boston: Beacon Press, 1994.
- Davids, Kenneth. *A Guide to Buying, Brewing and Enjoying,* San Francisco: 101 Production, 1979.
- Dawkins, Kristin. *Principles of Fair Trade and a Just Foreign Policy.* Penang: Third World Resurgence, 1993.
- De Cenival, Laure. "Commerce équitable, citoyenneté d'entreprise et des consommateurs." Paris: Sol@gral/FNDVA, 1997.
- Decornoy, Jacques. "Les voies et les moyens du commerce équitable." *Manière de voir.* No. 32 (November 1996): 80.
- Dewey, K. G. *Nutrition Consequences of the transfer from Subsistence to Commercial Agriculture in Tabasco: Food Energy in Tropical Ecosystems,* New York: Gordon and Breach Science Publisher. 105-144, 1985.
- Diaz, Ximena Avellaneda. *Los grupos etnicos del estado de Oaxaca.* América Indigena. Vol. 50. No. 2, 1990. 8-9.
- *Dictionary of International Law and Diplomacy.* (New York: Dobbs Ferry and Phonix Press inc. 1973).
- Dicum, Greg, and Nina Luttinger. *The Coffee Book: Anatomy of an industry from crop to the last drop.* New York: The New Press, 1999.
- Dijksterhuis, Koos. *Fair Trade: Guide to Good Practice.* The Hague: Towns & Development, 1995.

· Dyer, Gwynne. *Globalization of the Nation-State; Behind the Headlines.* Ottawa: Canadian Institute of International Affairs (1996).
· *Dow Jones International News.* Coffee Cos. Gain from Globalization but See Shortfalls. 21 May 2001.
· The Economist Intelligence Unit Limited. EIU Country Report 2nd quarter 1999, 5.
· Équiterre. *What is fair trade coffee? Fair Trade: A growing trend in the coffee industry.* Montréal: Équiterre, 2000.
· European Fair Trade Association (EFTA). *Fair trade in Europe: Facts and figures on the fair-trade sector in 16 European countries.* Maastricht: European Fair Trade Association, 1998.
· European Fair Trade Association. *Fair Trade Yearbook.* Maastricht: European Fair Trade Association, 1995.
· European Fair Trade Association. "Commerce équitable: Mémento pour l'an 2000." Maastricht: European Fair Trade Association, 1998.
· European Fair Trade Marking Movement. *Draft Opinion of the Section for External Relations, Trade and Development Policy on the European "fair trade" marking movement.* Brussels: European Fair Trade Marking Movement, November 24, 1995.
· FairTrade Labelling Organizations International. *Les conditions pour l'achat de café Max Havelaar/TransFair/FairTrade.* Utrecht: FairTrade Labelling Organizations International, June 1995.
· FairTrade Labelling Organizations International. "Commerce Équitable: Une alternative viable pour les petits planteurs." Utrecht: FairTrade Labelling Organizations International, April 1998.
· Fédération Artisans du Monde. *Échangeons le monde! Échangeons équitablement!* Paris: Fédération Artisans du Monde, 1999.
· Ferré, Felipe. *L'aventure du café.* Milan: Denoël, 1988.
· Giovannucci, Daniele. *Sustainable Coffee Survey of the North American Speciality Coffee Industry.* Conducted for the Summit Foundation, the Nature Conservancy, the North American Commission for Environmental Cooperation, the Speciality Coffee Association of America and the World Bank. May 2001.
· Greenberg, Russel, Peter Bichier, Andrea Angon Cruz, and Robert Reitsma. *Bird Populations in Shade and Sun Coffee Plantations in Central Guatemala.* Conservation Biology. Vol. 11 (April 1997): 448-459.
· Greenberg, Russel. *Birds in the Tropics, The Coffee Connection.* Birding (Washington, D.C.). December 1996: 472-481.

- Greenfield, Myrna. Alternative Trade: Giving Coffee a New Flavor: Making Coffee Strong, Equal Exchange: Boston, 1993, 7-12.
- Hawken, Paul. *The Ecology of Commerce: A declaration for sustainability.* New York: HarperBusiness, 1993.
- International Federation of Organic Agriculture Movement. *IFOAM position document on organic agriculture. Prepared for the FAO conference "Cultivating our Future."* Maastricht: IFOAM, September 12-17th 1999.
- James, Deborah. "Justice and Java: Coffee in a Fair Trade Market." *North American Congress on Latin America.* Vol. 34, No. 2 (October 2000).
- Johnson, Pierre-Marc, and Karel Mayrand. *Beyond Trade: The Case for a Broadened International Governance Agenda.* Montréal: Institute for Research on Public Policy, June 2000.
- Khor, Martin, "Global Economy and the Third World" in *The Case Against the Global Economy.* Sierra Club Books, San Francisco, 1996.
- Kirby, Alex. GM coffee "threatens farmers." BBC News Online. Thursday, 17 May, 2001.
- Klein, Naomi. *No Logo: Taking on the brand bullies.* Toronto: Vintage Canada. 2000.
- Korten, David C. *The Post Corporate World: Life After Capitalism.* San Francisco: Kumarian Press and Berrett-Koehler Publishers, 1999.
- Krier, Jean-Marie. *Fair Trade in Europe 2001.* Maastricht: European Fair Trade Association, 2001.
- Lehman, Karen "Au Mexique, les fausses promesses de l'Alena." *Le monde diplomatique.* November 1996, 26.
- Lumbanraja, J., T. Syam,. H. Nishide, A. K. Mahi, M. Utomo, and M. Kimura. *Deterioration of Soil Fertility by Land Use Changes in South Sumatra, Indonesia: from 1970-1990.* Hydrological Processes. October-November 1998: 2003-2013.
- Mallet, Patrick. *ISEAL Alliance Strategic Role: Background Paper.* Knowlesville: Falls Brook Centre, May 2001.
- Mander, Jerry, and Edward Goldsmith, ed. *The Case Against the Global Economy and for a turn toward the local.* San Francisco: Sierra Club Books, 1996.
- Max Havelaar France. "Vers un commerce plus juste: les consommateurs s'engagent." Paris: Max Havelaar France, April 1998.
- Max Havelaar Switzerland. *Max Havelaar Express.* Basle: Max Havelaar Switzerland, March 1998.

- Max Havelaar Switzerland. *Rapport annual 1996*. Basle: Max Havelaar Switzerland, 1996.
- M'Gonigle, Michael. *An Emerging Global Constitution. Focus on Forests and Communities*. The International Network of Forests and Communities, WTO Edition (Victoria), November 1999.
- McGrew, Antony. *The Transformation of Democracy*. Cambridge: Polity Press, 1997.
- McLean, Jennifer. *"Merging Ecological and Social Criteria for Agriculture: The Case of Coffee."* M.S. Research Paper. University of Maryland, December 1997.
- North American Free Trade Agreement Secretariat: www.nafta-sec-alena.org.
- O'Malley, Aiden, Angelo Caserta, Claudia Caldeirinha, Grazia Rita Pignatelli and Jim Brigham. *Fair Alternative with Integrated Rules: Toward a European Charter of Criteria for Fair Trade*. Rome: Anterem, 1998.
- Osmaòczyk, Edmund Jan. *Encyclopedia of the United Nations and International Agreements*. 2d ed. New York, Philadelphia and London: Taylor and Francis. 1990.
- Oxfam International. *Bitter Coffee: How the poor are paying for the slump in coffee prices*. Oxfam Policy Paper, Oxfam International, 2001.
- Pendergrast, Mark. *Uncommon Grounds: The History of Coffee and How It Transformed* Our World. New York: Basic Books, 1999. Oxfam International. Bitter Coffee: How the poor are paying for the slump in coffee prices. Oxfam Policy Paper, Oxfam International, 2001.
- Perfecto, I., and J. Vandermeer. *Microclimatic changes and the indirect loss of ant diversity in a tropical agroecosystem*. Oecologia 108 (November 1996): 577-582.
- Perfecto, I, J. Vandermeer, P. Hanson, and V. Cartin. *Arthropod biodiversity loss and the transformation of tropical agro-ecosystem*. Biodiversity and Conservation. Vol. 6 (July 1997): 935-945.
- Quebec Public Interest Research Group. *Hungry for Justice*. Montréal: Potluck Publishing, 1993.
- Rainforest Alliance. *Annual Report 2000*. New York: Rainforest Alliance, 2000.
- Rainforest Alliance. *The Conservation Coffee Campaign: Organizer's Kit*. New York: Rainforest Alliance, 1997.
- Ransom, David. "What's brewing," *The New Internationalist*. Vol. 271 (September 1995): 28-30.

- Rice, Paul D., and Jennifer McLean. *Sustainable Coffee at the Crossroads.* Washington, D.C.: Consumer's Choice Council, October 15, 1999.
- Rice, Robert A., and Justin R. Ward. *Coffee, Conservation, and Commerce in the Western Hemisphere.* Washington, D.C.: Smithsonian Migratory Bird Center, 1996.
- Ritchie, Mark. *Free Trade versus Sustainable Agriculture: The Implications of NAFTA.* The Ecologist. Vol.22, No. 5 (September-October 1992), 221-227.
- Robins, Nick, Robert, Sarah and Abbot, Jo. *Sustainable Trade: Who benefits?* International Institute for Environment and Development, 1999.
- Roseberry, William and Lowell Gudmundson, eds. *Coffee, Society, and Power in Latin America.* London: The Johns Hopkins University Press, 1995.
- Salazar, Hilda, and Laura Carlsen. *The social and environmental impacts of NAFTA: Grassroots responses to economic integration.* Mexico: Red Mexicana de Acción Frente al Libre Comercio, 2001.
- Sauvé, Mathieu-Robert. "Les bonnes actions." *L'Actualité* (Montréal). Vol. 26, No.2 (February 2001), 66.
- Second People's Summit. "Déclaration du Forum Environnement." Montréal: Regroupement Québécois des Groupes Écologistes, April 18, 2001.
- Seybold, Patricia B. *The Customer Revolution: How to thrive when customers are in control.* New York: Crown Business, 2001.
- Shrybman, Steven. *The World Trade Organization: A Citizen's Guide.* Ottawa: The Canadian Centre for Policy Alternatives, and Toronto: James Lorimer & Company, 1999.
- Smith, Adam. *An Inquiry into the Nature and Causes of the Wealth of Nations.* Oxford and New York: Oxford University Press, 1993.
- Smith, Linda Tuhiwai. *Decolonizing Methodologies: Research and Indigenous peoples.* London and New York: Zed Books, 1999.
- Speciality Coffee Association of America. *1999 Coffee Market Summary.* (Long Beach): Speciality Coffee Association of America, 1999.
- Statistic Canada. *Food consumption in Canada, Part 1, #32-229-XPB.* Ottawa: Minister of Industry, June 1999.
- Stringer, Ernest T. *Action Research.* 2d ed. Thousand Oaks, Sage Publications, 1999.
- Thomson, Bob. *Mexican farmers fight with fair prices, not guns: Food for Thought.* Ottawa: Transfair Canada, Fall 1994.
- Tortora, Gérard. *Principes d'anatomie et de physiologie,* Montréal: Centre Éducatif et Culturel, 1988.

- UCIRI. "¿Quienes somos?," *Nuestro Caminar,* Ixtepec: UCIRI. No. 28, November 1991.
- UCIRI. "Nuestra Historia:" *Nuestra Caminar,* Ixtepec: UCIRI. No. 27, 1991
- United Nations Conference on Trade and Development (UNCTD). *Coffee: An Exporter's Guide.* Geneva: United Nations, 1992.
- United Nations Conference on Trade and Development (UNCTD). *Commodity Yearbook 1995.* Geneva: United Nations, 1995.
- United Nations Development Program (UNDP). *Human Development Report 1999.* London: Oxford University Press, 1999.
- United Nations Development Program (UNDP). *Human Development Report 2000.* London: Oxford University Press, 2000.
- United States Department of Agriculture. *Tropical Products: World Markets and Trade.* Circular Series, FTROP 1-97 (Washington, D.C.), March 1997: 110.
- Van der Hoff, Franz. *Organizar la Esperanza,* Disertación pare obtener el grado de doctor en la Universidad Católica de Nimega, Uitgeversmaatschappij J. H. Kok, Kampen 1992.
- Wallach, Lori, and Michelle Sforza. *Whose Trade Organization?* Washington, D.C.: Public Citizen, 1999.
- Waridel, Laure and Sara Teitelbaum. *Fair Trade: Contributing to equitable commerce in Holland, Belgium, Switzerland, and France.* Montréal: Équiterre, 1999.
- *Webster's Encyclopedic Unabridged Dictionary of the English Language.* (New York: Gramercy Book. 1989).
- Wilson, Maureen G., and Elizabeth Whitmore. *Seeds of Fire: Social Development in an Era of Globalism.* Halifax: Fernwood Publishing, 2000.
- Wrigley, Gordon. *Coffee,* New York: Longman Scientific & Technical, 1988.

Online References

- Adbusters: www.adbusters.org
- Audubon: www.seattleaudubon.org/coffee
- Canadian International Development Agency (CIDA): www.acdi-cida.gc.ca
- Clean Clothes: www.cleanclothes.org/index.htm
- Codex Alimentarius Commission: www.fao.org/WAICENT/FAOINFO/ECO-NOMIC/ESN/codex/STANDARD/standard.htm
- Coffee Talk: www.halcyon.com/ctmag/0296/02/home.html
- Commission for Environmental Cooperation: www.cec.org
- Consumer's Choice Council: www.consumerscouncil.org
- Canadian Council for International Cooperation: www.fly.web.net/ccic-ccci
- Coop America's Sweatshop.org: www.sweatshops.org/
- Council on Economic Priorities: www-2.realaudio.com/CEP/home.html
- Corporate Watch: www.corpwatch.org/
- ECO-OK (certification): www.rainforest-alliance.org/programs/cap/program-description3.html
- Equal Exchange (USA): www.equalexchange.com
- Équiterre (Québec): www.equiterre.qc.ca
- Ethical Trading Initiative (ETI): www.ethicaltrade.org
- Fair Trade Foundation (UK): www.fairtrade.org.uk
- Global Exchange: www.globalexchange.org
- Human Rights Watch: www.hrw.org
- Institute for Agriculture and Trade Policy (IATP): www.iatp.iatp.org
- International Federation for Alternative Trade (IFAT): www.ifat.org
- International Coffee Organization: www.ico.org
- Natural Capitalism: www.naturalcapitalism.org
- Organic Consumers Association (OCA): www.organicconsumers.org
- Organic Trade Association (OTA): www.ota.com
- Oxfam America: www.oxfamamerica.org
- Oxfam Canada: www.oxfam.ca
- Oxfam International: www.oxfaminternational.org
- Oxfam Québec: www.oxfam.qc.ca
- Rural Advancement Foundation International (RAFI): ww.rafi.org
- Shared Interest: www.shared-interest.com
- Social Investment: www.socialinvestment.ca
- Smithsonian Migratory Bird Centre (shade certification): www.si.edu/resource/faq/nmnh/ecology.htm
- Specialty Coffee Association of America (SCAA): www.scaa.org
- Sustainable Harvest: www.sustainableharvest.com
- Ten Thousand Villages: www.villages.ca
- Transfair Canada (fair-trade certification): www.web.net/fairtrade
- Transfair USA (fair-trade certification): www.transfairusa.org
- United Nations Conference on Trade and Development (UNCTAD): www.unctad.org/
- United Nations Development Programme (UNDP): www.undp.org

Photographs by Éric St-Pierre

Index

JUST DOING IT
Popular Collective Action in the Americas
Gene Desfor, Deborah Barndt and Barbara Rahder, editors

Massive protests have disrupted global summit meetings from Seattle to Quebec City and from Gothenburg to Genoa. These demonstrations let the world know that resistance to globalization remains strong and vibrant. Not as clearly heard, though, are accounts of local communities organizing popular collective actions to resist those same institutions and policies of globalization.

Focusing on four countries—Mexico, Guatemala, United States, and Canada—and with the understanding that acts of resistance begin with the individual and move to communities, to cities, to regions and to nation-states, the narratives in this volume tell of peoples' collective struggles for environmental, economic and social justice.

These poignant and inspiring stories of communities taking action and successfully resisting the corporate agenda...eloquently told...reveal the strength and creativity of people living on the margins, from Santiago Atitlán in Guatemala to Vancouver, Canada.

> —Leonie Sandercock, School of Community and Regional Planning, University of British Columbia

Contributors include: Galit Wolfensohn, Egla Martinez-Salazar, Cindy McCulligh, Sheelagh Davis, W. Alexander Long, Emily Chan, Sarah Koch-Schulte, and Emilie K. Adin.

GENE DESFOR, DEBORAH BARNDT, and BARBARA RAHDER, teach in the Faculty of Environmental Studies at York University.

224 pages, photographs
Paperback ISBN: 1-55164-200-X $24.99
Hardcover ISBN: 1-55164-201-8 $53.99

BOOKS of RELATED INTEREST from

BLACK ROSE BOOKS